Building MATH FLUENCY

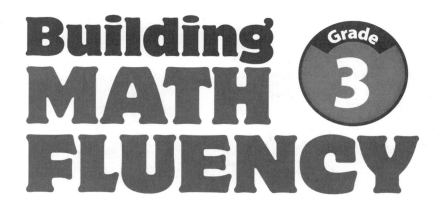

Grade 3

Consultant: Eleanor Falk Young
Editorial Development: Marilyn Evans
Copy Editing: Carrie Gwynne
Art Direction: Cheryl Puckett
Cover Design: Liliana Potigian
Illustration: Jo Larsen
Design/Production: Marcia Smith

Evan-Moor
EDUCATIONAL PUBLISHERS®
Helping Children Learn since 1979

EMC 3035

Congratulations on your purchase of some of the finest teaching materials in the world.

For information about other Evan-Moor products, call 1-800-777-4362, fax 1-800-777-4332, or visit our Web site, www.evan-moor.com. Entire contents © 2008 EVAN-MOOR CORP. 18 Lower Ragsdale Drive, Monterey, CA 93940-5746. Printed in USA.

Correlated to State Standards

Visit *teaching-standards.com* to view a correlation of this book's activities to your state's standards. This is a free service.

Contents

What's in This Book? 4

Glossary of Mathematics Terms 5

Addition

  Teaching Addition Strategies............... 6
  Addition Strategies............................. 7

Addition Strategies Practice

  Count Up.. 8
  Tens Partners 9
  Sums of 20....................................... 11
  Add with Tens Partners 12
  Doubles.. 13
  Doubles Plus 1, Doubles Plus 2 15
  Hidden Doubles 16
  Mixed Strategies Practice 17
  Plus 10.. 18
  Plus 10, Plus 20................................ 19
  Plus 9.. 20
  Plus 8.. 21
  Plus 19.. 22
  Plus 99.. 23
  Add in Small Steps 24
  Mixed Strategies Practice 25
  Sums to 20 Chart.............................. 27

Subtraction

  Teaching Subtraction Strategies.......... 29
  Subtraction Strategies 30

Subtraction Strategies Practice

  Count Back 31
  Count Up.. 32
  Mixed Strategies Practice 33
  Think Addition.................................. 34
  Tens Partners 36
  Doubles.. 37
  Minus 10 38
  Minus 10, Minus 20........................... 39
  Minus 9 40
  Minus 8 41
  Minus 19; Minus 99........................... 42
  Subtract in Small Steps 43
  Mixed Strategies Practice 45

Multiplication

  Teaching Multiplication Strategies........ 48
  Multiplication Strategies...................... 49

Multiplication Strategies Practice

  Counting Equal Groups 50
  Turn Around..................................... 51
  Times 0; Times 1 52
  Times 2... 53
  Times 3... 54
  Mixed Strategies Practice 57
  Times 10.. 60
  Times 4... 63
  Times 5... 66
  Mixed Strategies Practice 68
  Times 6... 69
  Multiples of 3 and 6........................... 71
  Times 7... 72
  Times 8... 74
  Multiples of 2, 4, and 8...................... 76
  Mixed Strategies Practice 77
  Times 9... 78
  Times 11.. 81
  Times 12.. 82
  Mixed Strategies Practice 83
  Square Numbers................................ 84
  Multiplication Table 86

Division

  Teaching Division Strategies 87
  Division Strategies 88

Division Strategies Practice

  Making Equal Groups 89
  Division of 0; Division by 1.................. 90
  A Number Divided by Itself 91
  Division by 2 92
  Division by 3 93
  Division by 2 and 3 94
  Division by 4 and 5 95
  Division by 6 and 7 96
  Division by 8 and 9 97
  Division by 10 and 11 98
  Division by 12 99
  Division with Remainders 100

Test Your Skills

  How to Use *Test Your Skills*................. 102

Building Math Fluency • EMC 3035 • © Evan-Moor Corp.

Addition Tests

Sums 0 to 10............................. 103

Sums 11 to 15 Test 1.......................... 104

Sums 11 to 15 Test 2.......................... 105

Sums 16 to 20.......................... 106

Sums to 20 Review 107

Subtraction Tests

Minuends to 10 108

Minuends 11 to 15 Test 1 109

Minuends 11 to 15 Test 2 110

Minuends 16 to 20 111

Minuends to 20 Review 112

Multiplication Tests

Products 0 to 10.............................. 113

Products 11 to 25 Test 1..................... 114

Products 11 to 25 Test 2..................... 115

Products 27 to 50 Test 1..................... 116

Products 27 to 50 Test 2..................... 117

Products 54 to 81 Test 1..................... 118

Products 54 to 81 Test 2..................... 119

Products 84 to 144.......................... 120

Products to 81 Review.......................... 121

Products to 144 Review....................... 122

Division Tests

Dividends 0 to 10................................. 123

Dividends 11 to 25 Test 1 124

Dividends 11 to 25 Test 2 125

Dividends 27 to 50 Test 1 126

Dividends 27 to 50 Test 2 127

Dividends 54 to 81 Test 1 128

Dividends 54 to 81 Test 2 129

Dividends 84 to 144 130

Dividends to 81 Review 131

Dividends to 144 Review 132

Student Practice Flashcards

How to Use Facts Flashcards.............. 133

Addition Flashcards 134

Subtraction Flashcards....................... 136

Multiplication Flashcards 138

Division Flashcards............................. 141

Flashcard Template 146

Answer Key.. 147

Transparencies ....Back of book

What's in This Book?

Mathematics standards frequently contain terminology such as "numerical fluency," "computational accuracy," and "automaticity." These terms recognize that the ability to compute quickly and accurately aids in higher-level mathematics and problem solving.

The goal of *Building Math Fluency* is to provide students with tools for thinking about computation in logical, strategic ways. Mastery of math facts is facilitated by understanding number relationships. Mastery is further enhanced with sufficient practice.

Strategy Practice

There is a section of strategy practice for each operation presented in this book. These practice pages can be done with students in a whole class or in small groups. Students benefit when teachers and peers model the use of the strategies and verbalize solution strategies aloud.

Charts of the strategies are presented both as reproducibles and as transparencies at the back of this book.

Practice pages feature a strategy box and problems to solve using that strategy.

Test Your Skills

The *Test Your Skills* pages provide concentrated facts practice. These pages can be used in a number of ways, as described on page 102. A feature of *Test Your Skills* is the opportunity for students to evaluate their own performance.

Facts Flashcards

Reproducible flashcards for the operations covered in this book are provided. The teacher resource page at the beginning of the section gives suggestions for using the cards to enhance students' mastery of number facts.

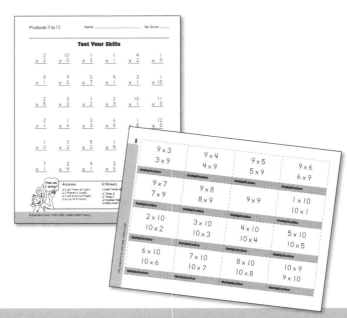

Glossary of Mathematics Terms

Addends The numbers in an addition problem.

$$3 + 4 = 7$$
addend   sum

Commutative Property of Addition Numbers can be added in any order without changing the sum.

$$3 + 4 = 7 \qquad 4 + 3 = 7$$

Commutative Property of Multiplication Factors can be multiplied in any order without changing the product.

$$3 \times 4 = 12 \qquad 4 \times 3 = 12$$

Difference The result of subtracting two numbers.

$$16 - 7 = 9$$
difference

Digit Any of the symbols 0, 1, 2, 3, 4, 5, 6, 7, 8, 9 used to write a number.

Fact Family A group of related facts, either addition and subtraction, or multiplication and division.

$$8 + 4 = 12 \qquad 4 + 8 = 12 \qquad 12 - 4 = 8 \qquad 12 - 8 = 4$$

Factors The numbers being multiplied.

$$3 \times 4 = 12$$
factor

Identity Property of Addition When 0 is added to a number, it does not change the total.

Identity Property of Multiplication The product of 1 and any number is that number.

$$1 \times 9 = 9 \qquad 49 \times 1 = 49$$

Minuend The number being subtracted from.

$$16 - 7 = 9$$
minuend

Multiples The product of a number and any whole number. For example, multiples of 4 are 0, 4, 8, 12, 16, etc.

Place Value The value of a digit as determined by its position in the ones place, tens place, etc. Each position is ten times of the place to its right and one-tenth of the place to its left.

Product The result of multiplication.

$$3 \times 4 = 12$$
product

Quotient The result of division.

$$12 \div 4 = 3$$
quotient

Subtrahend The number being subtracted.

$$16 - 7 = 9$$
subtrahend

Sum The result of joining quantities; the total.

$$3 + 4 = 7$$
sum

Teaching Addition Strategies

Pages 8–28 present practice with addition strategies that promote fact mastery and build computational fluency through focus on important number relationships and patterns.

Count Up An efficient strategy to use when adding a small quantity to a larger quantity. Students start with the larger addend and count up the smaller addend to find the sum.

Tens Partners Tens Partners are number pairs that make 10:

$0 + 10, \ 1 + 9, \ 2 + 8, \ 3 + 7, \ 4 + 6, \ 5 + 5$

Students can use Tens Partners when they are finding sums of 20.
For example: $12 + 8 = 10 + (2 + 8) = 10 + 10$

Doubles Facts in which an addend is added to itself (example: $4 + 4$). Students discover that Doubles have even sums. When students have learned the Doubles facts, they have an "anchor" from which to compute many other facts.

Doubles Plus 1 means double the addend and add one more.
Doubles Plus 2 means double the addend and add two more.

Doubles Fact	Doubles Plus 1	Doubles Plus 2
$6 + 6 = 12$	$6 + 7 = 13$	$6 + 8 = 14$

Plus 10 When 10 is added to a number, the tens-place digit increases by one, while the ones-place digit remains the same (example: $44 + 10 = \underline{5}4$).

Note: When adding 10 to a number that has a 9 in the tens place, you make 10 tens, or 100 (example: $94 + 10 = \underline{10}4$).

Plus 9 This strategy is based on the fact that 9 is one away from 10.

Plus 8 This strategy is based on the fact that 8 is two away from 10.

See 9. Think 10.	See 8. Think 10.
See $6 + 9$. Think $6 + 10 - 1$	See $6 + 8$. Think $6 + 10 - 2$

Add in Small Steps This strategy is based on the fact that it's easy to add a number to 10 or to a multiple of 10. Split the smaller addend into two parts, with one of those parts being the amount needed to make 10. For example:

$35 + 7 = 35 + 5 + 2 = 40 + 2 = 42$

Hidden Facts Find Tens Partners or Doubles hidden within problems to make computing easier.

	Hidden Tens Partners	Hidden Doubles
$7 + 5 = ?$	$7 + 3 + 2$	$6 + 6$
$6 + 8 = ?$	$6 + 4 + 4$ $8 + 2 + 4$	$6 + 6 + 2$ $7 + 7$

Addition Strategies

Count Up	Count up from the larger number. Use when adding on 1, 2, 3, or 4.
Tens Partners	There are six sets of number pairs that make 10: $\quad$ 10 + 0 $\qquad$ 9 + 1 $\qquad$ 8 + 2 $\quad$ 7 + 3 $\qquad$ 6 + 4 $\qquad$ 5 + 5 .... Tens Partners can be extended to the sums of 20. Make the ones-place digits Tens Partners. $\quad$ 12 + 8, 16 + 4
Doubles	Add the number to itself and that number doubles. $\quad$ 2 + 2 = 4 $\qquad$ 6 + 6 = 12
Doubles Plus 1	Double the number and add one more. If you know 7 + 7 = 14, then 7 + 8 is one more, or 15.
Doubles Plus 2	Double the number and add two more. If you know 5 + 5 = 10, then 5 + 7 is two more, or 12
Plus 10	When 10 is added to a number, the tens-place digit increases by one. $\quad$ 23 + 10 = 33
Plus 9 **See 9. Think 10.**	Add 10 and subtract 1. $\quad$ Example: 18 + 9 $\quad$ Think: 18 + 10 = 28 $\quad$ so $\quad$ 18 + 9 is one less, or 27. .... Plus 9 can be extended to Plus 19: Add 20 and subtract 1. Plus 9 can be extended to Plus 99: Add 100 and subtract 1.
Plus 8 **See 8. Think 10.**	Add 10 and subtract 2.
Add in Small Steps	Split the smaller number into two parts so that you can add up to a multiple of 10. For example: 26 + 7 = ? 1. The Tens Partner for **6** in **26** is 4. So, split 7 into 4 + 3. 2. Add the Tens Partners numbers: 26 + 4 = 30 3. Then add the remaining number: 30 + 3 = 33
Hidden Facts	Finding Tens Partners and Doubles hidden within problems can make the problems easier to solve.

Hidden Tens Partners	Hidden Doubles
8 + 6 = (8 + 2) + 4 $\quad$ = 10 + 4 $\quad$ = 14	6 + 8 = (6 + 6) + 2 $\quad$ = 12 + 2 $\quad$ = 14

Strategy

Count Up

Count Up from the larger number.
Use when adding on 1, 2, 3, or 4.

Add 1 or 2.

{10, 11}
9 + 2 = __11__

{13, 14}
12 + 2 = _____

15 + 2 = _____

8 + 2 = _____   28 + 2 = _____   19 + 2 = _____

59 + 1 = _____   79 + 2 = _____   109 + 1 = _____

2 + 88 = _____   1 + 149 = _____   263 + 2 = _____

Add 3 or 4.

{10, 11, 12}
9 + 3 = __12__

12 + 4 = _____   15 + 4 = _____

8 + 3 = _____   19 + 3 = _____   28 + 4 = _____

38 + 3 = _____   79 + 3 = _____   99 + 3 = _____

3 + 37 = _____   4 + 136 = _____   109 + 3 = _____

Strategy

Tens Partners

Number pairs that make 10 are called **Tens Partners**.

Write the number sentences that are possible for each ten frame.

_10_ + _0_ = 10

_0_ + _10_ = 10

_9_ + _1_ = 10

_____ + _____ = 10

_____ + _____ = 10

_____ + _____ = 10

_____ + _____ = 10

_____ + _____ = 10

_____ + _____ = 10

_____ + _____ = 10

_____ + _____ = 10

Close your eyes.
Say the number pairs that make 10.
Practice so that you learn them all.

10 and 0,
9 and 1,
8 and 2...

Addition 9

Strategy

Tens Partners

There are six **Tens Partners**.

Complete the **Tens Partners**.

$0 +$ _____ $= 10$ $3 +$ _____ $= 10$

$1 +$ _____ $= 10$ $4 +$ _____ $= 10$

$2 +$ _____ $= 10$ $5 +$ _____ $= 10$

Explain how you remember the **Tens Partners** number pairs.

_____

_____

Solve the **Tens Partners** problems. Leave the other problems blank.

$$
\begin{array}{ccccccc}
5 & 3 & 2 & 4 & 7 & 2 & 6 \\
+\,6 & +\,7 & +\,9 & +\,6 & +\,4 & +\,8 & +\,3 \\
\hline
\end{array}
$$

$$
\begin{array}{ccccccc}
6 & 9 & 3 & 5 & 2 & 9 & 6 \\
+\,6 & +\,1 & +\,8 & +\,5 & +\,7 & +\,2 & +\,4 \\
\hline
\end{array}
$$

 Building Math Fluency • EMC 3035 • © Evan-Moor Corp.

Name _____

Sums of 20

To find sums of 20, make the ones-place digits **Tens Partners**.

Use **Tens Partners** to make sums of 20.

11 + _____ = 20   14 + _____ = 20

17 + _____ = 20   15 + _____ = 20

16 + _____ = 20   18 + _____ = 20

13 + _____ = 20   20 + _____ = 20

19 + _____ = 20   12 + _____ = 20

Circle only the problems with sums of 20.

```
   12          13          12          14          11
 +  9        +  7        +  8        +  5        +  7
```

```
   15          11          16          14          17
 +  5        +  9        +  4        +  3        +  2
```

Strategy

Add with Tens Partners

Look for **Tens Partners** in addition problems with larger numbers.

Join the **Tens Partners**. Add.

$$34 + 6 = \underline{40}$$

- Join the Tens Partners. $4 + 6 = 10$
- Now add the 10 $30 + 10 = 40$

$17 + 3 = \underline{}$ $27 + 3 = \underline{}$ $57 + 3 = \underline{}$

$26 + 4 = \underline{}$ $96 + 4 = \underline{}$ $134 + 6 = \underline{}$

$19 + 1 = \underline{}$ $11 + 9 = \underline{}$ $101 + 9 = \underline{}$

Use the same strategy when both addends are multi-digit.

$$25 + 15 = \underline{40}$$

- First add the tens-place digits. $20 + 10 = 30$
- Then join the Tens Partners. $5 + 5 = 10$
- Now add the 10. $30 + 10 = 40$

Now try these.

$14 + 36 = \underline{}$ $27 + 63 = \underline{}$ $59 + 31 = \underline{}$

$65 + 35 = \underline{}$ $48 + 12 = \underline{}$ $78 + 22 = \underline{}$

Strategy

Doubles

When you add a number to itself, that's a **Double**.

Record the sums.

$1 + 1 = $ _____ $2 + 2 = $ _____

$3 + 3 = $ _____ $4 + 4 = $ _____

$5 + 5 = $ _____ $6 + 6 = $ _____

$7 + 7 = $ _____ $8 + 8 = $ _____

$9 + 9 = $ _____ $10 + 10 = $ _____

Describe the patterns you find in the sums.

_____

_____

Solve.

$11 + 11 = $ _____ $12 + 12 = $ _____ $13 + 13 = $ _____

$14 + 14 = $ _____ $15 + 15 = $ _____ $16 + 16 = $ _____

Addition   **13**

Strategy

Doubles

Use the **Doubles** strategy for larger numbers.

I know 4 + 4 = 8, so 40 + 40 = 80

Solve the **Doubles** facts.

10 + 10 = _____   60 + 60 = _____

20 + 20 = _____   70 + 70 = _____

30 + 30 = _____   80 + 80 = _____

40 + 40 = _____   90 + 90 = _____

50 + 50 = _____   100 + 100 = _____

I know 4 + 4 = 8, so 400 + 400 = 800

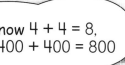

Solve the problems.

300 + 300 = _____   3,000 + 3,000 = _____

400 + 400 = _____   4,000 + 4,000 = _____

500 + 500 = _____   5,000 + 5,000 = _____

Name _____

Doubles Plus 1
Doubles Plus 2

When you know **Doubles**, you also know **Doubles Plus 1** and **Doubles Plus 2**.

Doubles: $5 + 5 = 10$ Double the number.
Doubles + 1: $5 + 6 = 11$ Double the number and add one more.
Doubles + 2: $5 + 7 = 12$ Double the number and add two more.

Complete the chart.

Doubles	Doubles + 1	Doubles + 2
$5 + 5 = $ _____	$5 + 6 = $ _____	$5 + 7 = $ _____
$6 + 6 = $ _____	$6 + 7 = $ _____	$6 + 8 = $ _____
$7 + 7 = $ _____	$7 + 8 = $ _____	$7 + 9 = $ _____
$8 + 8 = $ _____	$8 + 9 = $ _____	$8 + 10 = $ _____
$9 + 9 = $ _____	$9 + 10 = $ _____	$9 + 11 = $ _____
$10 + 10 = $ _____	$10 + 11 = $ _____	$10 + 12 = $ _____
$12 + 12 = $ _____	$12 + 13 = $ _____	$12 + 14 = $ _____
$15 + 15 = $ _____	$15 + 16 = $ _____	$15 + 17 = $ _____
$20 + 20 = $ _____	$20 + 21 = $ _____	$20 + 22 = $ _____

Strategy

Hidden Doubles

Look for **Doubles** hidden in a problem. Then decide how many more to add.

Doubles + 1	Look for the Doubles.	How many more?	Sum
5 + 6	5 + 5	+ 1	11
6 + 7			
8 + 9			
7 + 8			

Doubles + 2	Look for the Doubles.	How many more?	Sum
4 + 6	4 + 4	+ 2	10
5 + 7			
6 + 8			
7 + 9			
Write your own:			

Building Math Fluency • EMC 3035 • © Evan-Moor Corp.

Name _____

Find the Sums

Use **Tens Partners** and **Doubles** facts to solve.

Tens Partners

7 + 3 = _____

17 + 3 = _____

17 + 13 = _____

5 + 5 = _____

15 + 5 = _____

15 + 15 = _____

25 + 15 = _____

8 + 2 = _____

18 + 2 = _____

18 + 12 = _____

28 + 12 = _____

28 + _____ = 50

Doubles Facts

2 + 2 = _____

22 + 2 = _____

22 + 22 = _____

3 + 3 = _____

33 + 3 = _____

33 + 33 = _____

333 + 33 = _____

4 + 4 = _____

44 + 4 = _____

44 + 44 = _____

444 + 44 = _____

444 + _____ = 888

Plus 10

It's easy to add 10.
Can you describe the pattern?

Add 10.

Number	Number + 10
4	14
14	
34	
54	
24	
74	
64	
84	

What happens to a number's
tens-place digit when you add 10?

_____

_____

_____

Add 10.

Number	Number + 10
93	
94	

What happens when you add 10 to a
number that has 9 in its tens place?

_____

_____

Find the sums.

$$\begin{array}{r} 35 \\ +\ 10 \\ \hline \end{array} \qquad \begin{array}{r} 89 \\ +\ 10 \\ \hline \end{array} \qquad \begin{array}{r} 93 \\ +\ 10 \\ \hline \end{array} \qquad \begin{array}{r} 107 \\ +\ 10 \\ \hline \end{array} \qquad \begin{array}{r} 152 \\ +\ 10 \\ \hline \end{array} \qquad \begin{array}{r} 193 \\ +\ 10 \\ \hline \end{array}$$

Building Math Fluency • EMC 3035 • © Evan-Moor Corp.

Strategy

Plus 10, Plus 20

When you add 10, the tens-place digit increases by one. When you add 20, the tens-place digit increases by two.

Plus 10

14 + 10 = _____

36 + 10 = _____

57 + 10 = _____

62 + 10 = _____

99 + 10 = _____

_____ + 10 = _____

Plus 20

14 + 20 = _____

36 + 20 = _____

57 + 20 = _____

62 + 20 = _____

99 + 20 = _____

_____ + 20 = _____

Solve the **Plus 100** problems.

To add 100, increase the _____s-place digit by one.

140 + 100 = _____   360 + 100 = _____

570 + 100 = _____   620 + 100 = _____

Now solve the **Plus 200** problems.

140 + 200 = _____   360 + 200 = _____

570 + 200 = _____   620 + 200 = _____

Strategy

Plus 9

See 9. Think 10.
It's easy to add 10.
For **Plus 9**, add 10 and subtract 1.

14 + 9 = ?
I know 14 + 10 = 24,
so 14 + 9 is one less.
24 − 1 = 23

Add. Use **See 9. Think 10**.

14 + 9 = __23__   38 + 9 = _____

17 + 9 = _____   42 + 9 = _____

26 + 9 = _____   45 + 9 = _____

18 + 9 = _____   65 + 9 = _____

25 + 9 = _____   76 + 9 = _____

37 + 9 = _____   88 + 9 = _____

What happens to a number's ones-place digit when you add 9?

_____

_____

Strategy

Plus 8

See 8. Think 10.
It's easy to add 10.
For **Plus 8**, add 10 and subtract 2.

16 + 8 = ?
I know 16 + 10 = 26,
so 16 + 8 is two less.
26 − 2 = 24

Add. Use **See 8. Think 10**.

16 + 8 = __24__   27 + 8 = _____   36 + 8 = _____

29 + 8 = _____   35 + 8 = _____   47 + 8 = _____

Add. Use three strategies.

Plus 10	**Plus 9**	**Plus 8**
38 + 10 = _____	38 + 9 = _____	38 + 8 = _____
55 + 10 = _____	55 + 9 = _____	55 + 8 = _____
49 + 10 = _____	49 + 9 = _____	49 + 8 = _____

Strategy

Plus 19

See 19. Think 20.
It's easy to add 20.
For **Plus 19**, add 20 and subtract 1.

$$35 + 19 = (35 + 20) - 1 = 55 - 1 = 54$$

Add 20 and subtract 1.

$27 + 19 =$ $(27 + 20) - 1 = 47 - 1 = 46$

$48 + 19 =$ _____

$64 + 19 =$ _____

$39 + 19 =$ _____

$70 + 19 =$ _____

Is the missing addend 19 or 20?

25	25	71	58	36
+☐	+☐	+☐	+☐	+☐
45	44	90	78	55

Write and solve your own **Plus 19** problem. Show your work.

_____ + _____ = _____

Strategy

Plus 99

See 99. Think 100.
It's easy to add 100. For Plus 99,
add 100 and subtract 1.

62 + 99 = ?
I know 62 + 100 = 162,
so 62 + 99 is one less.
162 − 1 = 161

Add 100 and subtract 1. Show your work.

45 + 99 = _____

19 + 99 = _____

52 + 99 = _____

37 + 99 = _____

Now solve these problems. Add 100 and subtract 1.

$$\begin{array}{r} 35 \\ + 99 \\ \hline \end{array} \qquad \begin{array}{r} 76 \\ + 99 \\ \hline \end{array} \qquad \begin{array}{r} 28 \\ + 99 \\ \hline \end{array} \qquad \begin{array}{r} 66 \\ + 99 \\ \hline \end{array}$$

Write and solve a **Plus 99** problem of your own.

_____

Strategy

Add in Small Steps

Split the smaller number into two parts so that you can add up to a multiple of 10 (20, 30, 40...).

26 + 7 = __33__

The Tens Partner for the **6** in **26** is 4.
I'll split 7 into 4 + 3.
Now I add 26 + 4. That's 30.
30 + 3 = 33
Wow! That's a snap!

Add in small steps.
First look for hidden **Tens Partners**.
Show your work.

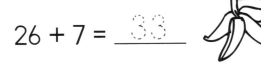

17 + 6 = __17 + (3 + 3) = 20 + 3 = 23_____

18 + 4 = _____

17 + 5 = _____

28 + 5 = _____

49 + 4 = _____

64 + 7 = _____

Mixed Strategies Practice

Name _____

Which Strategy Fits?

Doubles   Doubles + 1   Doubles + 2   ~~Tens Partners~~   Plus 10   Plus 9

Solve the problems.
Write the strategy name.

Strategy name
Tens Partners

1 + 9 = _____
4 + 6 = _____
5 + 5 = _____
7 + 3 = _____
2 + 8 = _____
10 + 0 = _____

Strategy name

7 + 10 = _____
4 + 10 = _____
5 + 10 = _____
17 + 10 = _____
26 + 10 = _____
48 + 10 = _____

Strategy name

7 + 9 = _____
4 + 9 = _____
5 + 9 = _____
17 + 9 = _____
26 + 9 = _____
48 + 9 = _____

Strategy name

6 + 6 = _____
7 + 7 = _____
8 + 8 = _____
9 + 9 = _____
12 + 12 = _____
25 + 25 = _____

Strategy name

6 + 7 = _____
7 + 8 = _____
8 + 9 = _____
9 + 10 = _____
12 + 13 = _____
25 + 26 = _____

Strategy name

7 + 9 = _____
8 + 10 = _____
6 + 8 = _____
5 + 7 = _____
12 + 14 = _____
25 + 27 = _____

Name _____

Many Ways to Add

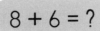

$$8 + 6 = ?$$

Think about which strategy makes sense to you.

I see **Tens Partners**.

I split 6 into 2 + 4

$8 + 6 = 8 + 2 + 4$
$= 10 + 4$
$= 14$

I see **Doubles**.

$6 + 6$

$6 + 8 = 6 + 6 + 2$
$= 12 + 2$
$= 14$

Think about the problems. Choose a strategy. Show your work.

What is your strategy for

$7 + 9 = ?$

My strategy was _____.

What is your strategy for

$18 + 6 = ?$

My strategy was _____.

Building Math Fluency • EMC 3035 • © Evan-Moor Corp.

Sums to 20 Chart

Write all the possible ways to make sums up to 20 using two addends.
Record up to two equations per box.
For each row, start with Plus 0 facts, then Plus 1 facts, and so on.

Sum	Combination of Two Addends								
0	0+0								
1	0+1 1+0								
2	0+2 2+0	1+1							
3									
4									
5									
6									
7									
8	0+8 8+0	1+7 7+1	2+6 6+2	3+5 5+3	4+4				

Combination of Two Addends (continued)

Sum	0+9 9+0	1+8 8+1	2+7 7+2	3+6 6+3	4+5 5+4					
9										
10										
11										
12										
13										
14										
15										
16										
17										
18										
19										
20										

Bonus: What is the total number of ways to make sums to 20 using two addends? _____

Teaching Subtraction Strategies

Pages 31–47 present practice with subtraction strategies that promote computational fluency and fact mastery.

There are two ways to look at subtraction:

- as the reduction of an amount
  "If I take 7 away from 16, I have 9 left."

- as the comparison of two quantities
  "The difference between 16 and 7 is 9."

$$\overset{\text{minuend}}{\underset{\text{subtrahend}}{16 - 7}} = 9 \leftarrow \text{difference}$$

Count Back	Also thought of as *take away*. This strategy is best when subtracting a small number (1, 2, or 3) from a larger number.
	For $19 - 2$, start at 19 and count back 2 to get to 17.
Count Up	Count up from the lower number to find the difference between the two quantities. This strategy is best when the minuend and subtrahend are close together.
	For $99 - 97$, count up 2 from 97 to 99.
Think Addition	Turn subtraction into addition problems. Students usually master addition facts first. This strategy allows them to use facts they know to compute new facts.
	Turn $17 - 12 = \square$ into $\square + 12 = 17$. Think: *What* $+ 12$ is 17?
Tens Partners	If you know the sums of 10 (Tens Partners), then you know the related subtraction facts:
	$10 - 9 = 1$ $10 - 8 = 2$ $10 - 7 = 3$
Doubles	If you know addition Doubles, then you know the related subtraction facts:
	$18 - 9 = 9$ $16 - 8 = 8$ $14 - 7 = 7$
Minus 10 Minus 9 Minus 8	Just as students learn patterns with Plus 10, they apply the opposite patterns to Minus 10. This can be extended to Minus 9 and Minus 8:
	See 9. Think 10. See $16 - 9$. Think $16 - 10$ and add 1.
	See 8. Think 10. See $15 - 8$. Think $15 - 10$ and add 2.
Subtract in Small Steps	This strategy is based on the fact that it's easy to subtract from 10 or a multiple of 10. Split the subtrahend into two parts, with one of those parts being the amount you need to subtract to get to a multiple of 10. For example:
	For $15 - 6$ try $15 - 5 - 1$
	For $24 - 7$ try $24 - 4 - 3$

Subtraction Strategies

Count Back	Count back to take away small numbers, such as 1, 2, or 3.
Count Up	Count up to find the difference. This works best when the numbers are close together. $11 - 9 = \square$ Count up from 9 to 11.
Think Addition	To subtract, think of the related addition fact. $13 - 6 = \square$ Think: $\square + 6 = 13$
Tens Partners	If you know the addition Tens Partners, then you know the related subtraction facts. $7 + 3 = 10$ so $10 - 3 = 7$ and $10 - 7 = 3$ .... Tens Partners can be extended to find differences from 20. $20 - 8 = 12$
Doubles	If you know the addition Doubles facts, then you know the related subtraction facts. $2 + 2 = 4$ so $4 - 2 = 2$
Minus 10	The tens-place digit decreases by one, and the ones-place digit stays the same. $23 - 10 = 13$
Minus 9 **See 9. Think 10.**	Subtract 10 and add 1. .... Minus 9 can be extended to Minus 19: Subtract 20 and add 1. Minus 9 can be extended to Minus 99: Subtract 100 and add 1.
Minus 8 **See 8. Think 10.**	Subtract 10 and add 2.
Subtract in Small Steps	Split the number being subtracted into two parts so that you can subtract to 10 or a multiple of 10. For example: $24 - 7 = \square$ $24 - 4 = 20$. So, split 7 into 4 and 3. Then apply Tens Partners to subtract 3 from 20. $20 - 3 = 17$

  Building Math Fluency • EMC 3035 • © Evan-Moor Corp.

Strategy

Count Back

Count Back to take away small numbers, such as 1, 2, or 3.

A number line can help you count back.

$19 - 2 = 17$

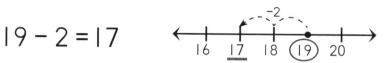

Start at 19, hop back 2, and land on 17.

Count Back to subtract.

(19, 18)

$20 - 2 = \underline{18}$

$18 - 1 = \underline{}$

$14 - 2 = \underline{}$

(16, 15)

$17 - 2 = \underline{}$

$11 - 2 = \underline{}$

$16 - 0 = \underline{}$

(18, 17, 16)

$19 - 3 = \underline{}$

$9 - 3 = \underline{}$

$12 - 3 = \underline{}$

Now solve these problems.

(81, 80, 79)

$82 - 3 = \underline{}$

$61 - 2 = \underline{}$

$40 - 2 = \underline{}$

$100 - 1 = \underline{}$

$55 - 2 = \underline{}$

$72 - 3 = \underline{}$

Fill in the missing number.

$38 - \boxed{} = 35$

$11 - \boxed{} = 9$

$20 - \boxed{} = 18$

$14 - \boxed{} = 11$

$12 - \boxed{} = 9$

$19 - \boxed{} = 16$

Strategy

Count Up

Count Up to find the difference. This works best when the numbers are close together.

A number line can help you count up.

$19 - 17 = 2$

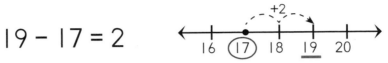

Start at 17 and count up to 19.

Count Up from the bottom number to find the difference.

$$\begin{array}{r} 16 \\ -14 \\ \hline \end{array} \qquad \begin{array}{r} 13 \\ -11 \\ \hline \end{array} \qquad \begin{array}{r} 20 \\ -17 \\ \hline \end{array} \qquad \begin{array}{r} 12 \\ -10 \\ \hline \end{array}$$

$$\begin{array}{r} 15 \\ -12 \\ \hline \end{array} \qquad \begin{array}{r} 19 \\ -18 \\ \hline \end{array} \qquad \begin{array}{r} 19 \\ -16 \\ \hline \end{array} \qquad \begin{array}{r} 11 \\ -\ 9 \\ \hline \end{array}$$

$$\begin{array}{r} 21 \\ -19 \\ \hline \end{array} \qquad \begin{array}{r} 22 \\ -19 \\ \hline \end{array} \qquad \begin{array}{r} 30 \\ -28 \\ \hline \end{array} \qquad \begin{array}{r} 45 \\ -43 \\ \hline \end{array}$$

Count Up to find the difference between the two numbers.

$18 - 16 =$ _____ $12 - 11 =$ _____ $12 - 9 =$ _____

$14 - 12 =$ _____ $16 - 15 =$ _____ $17 - 14 =$ _____

$27 - 25 =$ _____ $30 - 29 =$ _____ $32 - 29 =$ _____

   Building Math Fluency • EMC 3035 • © Evan-Moor Corp.

Name _____

Which Strategy Fits?

Count Back

Count back to take away small numbers like 1, 2, or 3.

$100 - 2 =$ ___98___

It is easy to count back 2 for this problem.

Count Up

Count up to find the difference between numbers that are close together.

$100 - 97 =$ ___3___

It is too far to count back 97. Count up from 97 to find the difference.

- -

Circle **Count Back** problems in red.
Circle **Count Up** problems in blue.
Solve all the problems.

$80 - 1 =$ _____ $101 - 1 =$ _____ $31 - 2 =$ _____

$80 - 78 =$ _____ $101 - 98 =$ _____ $31 - 29 =$ _____

$99 - 2 =$ _____ $59 - 58 =$ _____ $90 - 3 =$ _____

Write an example of each type of problem.

Count Back	Count Up

Strategy

Think Addition

To subtract, think of the related addition fact.

Instead of subtracting, I add.

$13 - 9 = ?$

Think $? + 9 = 13$

That's $4 + 9 = 13$

Think of the related addition fact to subtract.

$17 - 12 = \underline{\quad}$ $20 - 14 = \underline{\quad}$ $15 - 9 = \underline{\quad}$

$11 - 7 = \underline{\quad}$ $19 - 9 = \underline{\quad}$ $12 - 7 = \underline{\quad}$

$15 - 11 = \underline{\quad}$ $16 - 8 = \underline{\quad}$ $13 - 6 = \underline{\quad}$

$$\begin{array}{r} 17 \\ -10 \\ \hline \end{array} \qquad \begin{array}{r} 16 \\ -11 \\ \hline \end{array} \qquad \begin{array}{r} 15 \\ -12 \\ \hline \end{array} \qquad \begin{array}{r} 14 \\ -8 \\ \hline \end{array}$$

$$\begin{array}{r} 13 \\ -7 \\ \hline \end{array} \qquad \begin{array}{r} 12 \\ -6 \\ \hline \end{array} \qquad \begin{array}{r} 11 \\ -8 \\ \hline \end{array} \qquad \begin{array}{r} 10 \\ -5 \\ \hline \end{array}$$

Strategy

Think Addition

To subtract, think of the related addition fact.

Solve and match the facts.

$16 - 14 =$ ___2___

$11 - 8 =$ _____

$14 - 7 =$ _____

$15 - 8 =$ _____

$13 - 8 =$ _____

$18 - 9 =$ _____

$15 - 9 =$ _____

$20 - 6 =$ _____

• $3 +$ _____ $= 11$

• $2 +$ __14__ $= 16$

• $7 +$ _____ $= 14$

• $7 +$ _____ $= 15$

• $9 +$ _____ $= 18$

• $5 +$ _____ $= 13$

• $14 +$ _____ $= 20$

• $6 +$ _____ $= 15$

Write three related addition and subtraction facts.

Example: $17 + 3 = 20$ and $20 - 3 = 17$

_____

_____

_____

Strategy

Tens Partners

Knowing the **Tens Partners** can help you solve subtraction problems.

Warm-Up

Write the six different **Tens Partners**.

$\underline{10} + \underline{0} = 10$ $\underline{} + \underline{} = 10$ $\underline{} + \underline{} = 10$

$\underline{} + \underline{} = 10$ $\underline{} + \underline{} = 10$ $\underline{} + \underline{} = 10$

Use **Tens Partners** to solve the subtraction problems.

$10 - 7 = \underline{}$ $10 - 3 = \underline{}$ $10 - 5 = \underline{}$

$10 - 4 = \underline{}$ $10 - 8 = \underline{}$ $10 - 9 = \underline{}$

$10 - 2 = \underline{}$ $10 - 1 = \underline{}$ $10 - 6 = \underline{}$

Now solve these problems.

$20 - 15 = \underline{}$ $20 - 17 = \underline{}$ $20 - 11 = \underline{}$

$20 - 13 = \underline{}$ $20 - 3 = \underline{}$ $20 - 9 = \underline{}$

$20 - 12 = \underline{}$ $20 - 14 = \underline{}$ $20 - 16 = \underline{}$

$100 - 70 = \underline{}$ $100 - 75 = \underline{}$ $100 - 55 = \underline{}$

Strategy

Doubles

Knowing **Doubles** can help you solve subtraction problems.

Warm-Up

Write the **Doubles** for each sum.

_5_ + _5_ = 10   ___ + ___ = 12   ___ + ___ = 14

___ + ___ = 16   ___ + ___ = 18   ___ + ___ = 20

Use **Doubles** facts to subtract.

20 – 10 = _____   16 – 8 = _____   12 – 6 = _____

14 – 7 = _____   18 – 9 = _____   10 – 5 = _____

$$\begin{array}{r} 16 \\ -\ 8 \\ \hline \end{array} \qquad \begin{array}{r} 12 \\ -\ 6 \\ \hline \end{array} \qquad \begin{array}{r} 14 \\ -\ 7 \\ \hline \end{array} \qquad \begin{array}{r} 18 \\ -\ 9 \\ \hline \end{array}$$

Now solve these **Doubles** subtraction problems.

100 – 50 = _____   60 – 30 = _____   80 – 40 = _____

50 – 25 = _____   30 – 15 = _____   24 – 12 = _____

Fill in the missing numbers.

42 – ___ = ___   28 – ___ = ___   64 – ___ = ___
    ↑   ↑   ↑   ↑   ↑   ↑
same number   same number   same number

Minus 10

Name _____

It's easy to subtract 10.
Can you describe the pattern?

Subtract 10.

Number	Number −10
54	44
34	
84	
24	
44	
64	
94	
74	

What happens to a number when 10 is subtracted?

_____

_____

_____

_____

Subtract.

$$\begin{array}{r} 15 \\ -10 \\ \hline \end{array} \qquad \begin{array}{r} 19 \\ -10 \\ \hline \end{array} \qquad \begin{array}{r} 20 \\ -10 \\ \hline \end{array} \qquad \begin{array}{r} 14 \\ -10 \\ \hline \end{array} \qquad \begin{array}{r} 17 \\ -10 \\ \hline \end{array} \qquad \begin{array}{r} 13 \\ -10 \\ \hline \end{array}$$

$$\begin{array}{r} 45 \\ -10 \\ \hline \end{array} \qquad \begin{array}{r} 79 \\ -10 \\ \hline \end{array} \qquad \begin{array}{r} 30 \\ -10 \\ \hline \end{array} \qquad \begin{array}{r} 64 \\ -10 \\ \hline \end{array} \qquad \begin{array}{r} 87 \\ -10 \\ \hline \end{array} \qquad \begin{array}{r} 93 \\ -10 \\ \hline \end{array}$$

Strategy

Minus 10, Minus 20

When you subtract 10, the tens-place digit decreases by one. When you subtract 20, the tens-place digit decreases by two.

Minus 10

14 – 10 = _____

36 – 10 = _____

57 – 10 = _____

62 – 10 = _____

99 – 10 = _____

Minus 20

44 – 20 = _____

56 – 20 = _____

87 – 20 = _____

92 – 20 = _____

99 – 20 = _____

Solve the **Minus 100** problems.

To subtract 100, decrease the _____s-place digit by one.

140 – 100 = _____   360 – 100 = _____

570 – 100 = _____   620 – 100 = _____

Now solve the **Minus 200** problems.

340 – 200 = _____   460 – 200 = _____

570 – 200 = _____   820 – 200 = _____

Strategy

Minus 9

See 9. Think 10.
It's easy to subtract 10. For Minus 9, subtract 10 and add 1.

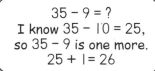

35 − 9 = ?
I know 35 − 10 = 25,
so 35 − 9 is one more.
25 + 1 = 26

Subtract. Use **See 9. Think 10.**

35 − 9 = __26__   38 − 9 = _____

37 − 9 = _____   42 − 9 = _____

26 − 9 = _____   45 − 9 = _____

28 − 9 = _____   65 − 9 = _____

25 − 9 = _____   75 − 9 = _____

17 − 9 = _____   88 − 9 = _____

What happens to a number's ones-place digit when you subtract 9?

_____

_____

Strategy

Minus 8

See 8. Think 10.
It's easy to subtract 10. For
Minus 8, subtract 10 and add 2.

35 − 8 = ?
I know 35 − 10 = 25,
so 35 − 8 is two more.
25 + 2 = 27

Subtract. Use **See 8. Think** 10.

35 − 8 = _27_   45 − 8 = _____   36 − 8 = _____

24 − 8 = _____   25 − 8 = _____   47 − 8 = _____

Subtract. Use three strategies.

Minus 10	**Minus 9**	**Minus 8**
37 − 10 = _____	37 − 9 = _____	37 − 8 = _____
55 − 10 = _____	55 − 9 = _____	55 − 8 = _____
42 − 10 = _____	42 − 9 = _____	42 − 8 = _____

Strategy

Minus 19

See 19. Think 20.
It's easy to subtract 20. For Minus 19, subtract 20 and add 1.

$$45 - 19 = (45 - 20) + 1 = 25 + 1 = 26$$

Try it.

$67 - 19 = \underline{(67 - 20) + 1 = 47 + 1 = 48}$

$48 - 19 = $ _____

$74 - 19 = $ _____

$56 - 19 = $ _____

Strategy

Minus 99

See 99. Think 100.
Think 100 to solve **Minus 99** problems. Subtract 100 and add 1.

$260 - 99 = \underline{(260 - 100) + 1 = 160 + 1 = 161}$

$240 - 99 = $ _____

$370 - 99 = $ _____

$480 - 99 = $ _____

Building Math Fluency • EMC 3035 • © Evan-Moor Corp.

Strategy

Subtract in Small Steps

Split the number you are subtracting into two parts so that you can subtract down to a 10. Then think **Tens Partners** to get the answer.

Subtracting in small steps is easier than it sounds.
Look below.

Split 6 into 5 and 1. Subtract 5 first to reach 10.

15 − 6 = ?
Subtract 6 in two steps: first −5 and then −1.

$$15 - 6 = 15 - 5 - 1$$
$$= 10 - 1$$
$$= 9$$

Split 7 into 4 and 3. Subtract 4 first to reach 20.

24 − 7 = ?
Subtract 7 in two steps: first −4 and then −3.

$$24 - 7 = 24 - 4 - 3$$
$$= 20 - 3$$
$$= 17$$

Split 8 into 6 and 2. Subtract 6 first to reach 20.

26 − 8 = ?
Subtract 8 in two steps: first −6 and then −2.

$$26 - 8 = 26 - \boxed{} - 2$$
$$= \underline{\qquad}$$
$$= \underline{\qquad}$$

Strategy

Subtract in Small Steps

Split the number you are subtracting into two parts so that you can subtract down to a 10. Then think **Tens Partners** to get the answer.

Subtract in small steps.

−2 and −2
22 − 4 = 18

−5 and −1
25 − 6 = _____

−3 and −1
13 − 4 = _____

and
24 − 6 = _____

and
21 − 4 = _____

and
14 − 5 = _____

and
26 − 7 = _____

and
22 − 5 = _____

and
24 − 7 = _____

and
34 − 8 = _____

and
42 − 7 = _____

and
52 − 4 = _____

and
104 − 8 = _____

and
106 − 7 = _____

and
202 − 5 = _____

Can you think of a better name for this strategy? Explain.

_____

_____

_____

Mixed Strategies Practice

Name _____

Which Strategy Fits?

======== Strategy Names ========

Count Back	Doubles	Minus 10
Minus 9	Tens Partners	~~Think Addition~~

Solve the problems.
Write the strategy name.

Strategy name
Think Addition

$17 - 9 =$ _____
$20 - 5 =$ _____
$15 - 6 =$ _____
$10 - 3 =$ _____
$11 - 7 =$ _____
$16 - 11 =$ _____

Strategy name

$17 - 10 =$ _____
$14 - 10 =$ _____
$15 - 10 =$ _____
$27 - 10 =$ _____
$36 - 10 =$ _____
$48 - 10 =$ _____

Strategy name

$17 - 9 =$ _____
$14 - 9 =$ _____
$15 - 9 =$ _____
$27 - 9 =$ _____
$36 - 9 =$ _____
$48 - 9 =$ _____

Strategy name

$10 - 6 =$ _____
$10 - 7 =$ _____
$10 - 8 =$ _____
$10 - 9 =$ _____
$10 - 3 =$ _____
$10 - 4 =$ _____

Strategy name

$14 - 7 =$ _____
$16 - 8 =$ _____
$18 - 9 =$ _____
$8 - 4 =$ _____
$12 - 6 =$ _____
$6 - 3 =$ _____

Strategy name

$11 - 2 =$ _____
$22 - 3 =$ _____
$18 - 1 =$ _____
$12 - 3 =$ _____
$19 - 1 =$ _____
$21 - 2 =$ _____

Name _____

Which Strategy Fits?

Strategy Names

| Minus 20 | Doubles | Minus 10 |
| Minus 9 | Tens Partners | ~~Count Up~~ |

Solve the problems.
Write the strategy name.

Strategy name

40 – 20 = _____
22 – 11 = _____
60 – 30 = _____
26 – 13 = _____
48 – 24 = _____
88 – 44 = _____

Strategy name

38 – 9 = _____
95 – 9 = _____
51 – 9 = _____
77 – 9 = _____
23 – 9 = _____
86 – 9 = _____

Strategy name

87 – 20 = _____
99 – 20 = _____
25 – 20 = _____
64 – 20 = _____
33 – 20 = _____
58 – 20 = _____

Strategy name

82 – 10 = _____
66 – 10 = _____
19 – 10 = _____
47 – 10 = _____
50 – 10 = _____
75 – 10 = _____

Strategy name
Count Up

22 – 19 = _____
40 – 37 = _____
15 – 12 = _____
25 – 23 = _____
31 – 28 = _____
51 – 49 = _____

Strategy name

10 – 9 = _____
10 – 7 = _____
20 – 12 = _____
20 – 9 = _____
10 – 4 = _____
20 – 16 = _____

Building Math Fluency • EMC 3035 • © Evan-Moor Corp.

Mixed Strategies Practice

Many Ways to Subtract

$$26 - 9 = ?$$

Think about which strategy makes sense to you.

See 9. Think 10.
I subtract 10 and add 1.

so

$$26 - 9 = 26 - 10 + 1$$
$$= 16 + 1$$
$$= 17$$

Subtract in Small Steps.
I split 9 into 6 and 3.

so

$$26 - 9 = 26 - 6 - 3$$
$$= 20 - 3$$
$$= 17$$

Think about the problems. Choose a strategy. Show your work.

What is your strategy for $18 - 9 = ?$

My strategy was _____.

What is your strategy for $14 - 8 = ?$

My strategy was _____.

Teaching Multiplication Strategies

Pages 50–86 present practice with multiplication strategies that promote computational fluency and fact mastery. Multiplication facts are introduced sequentially with the exception of Times 10, which is presented after Times 3 because Times 10 facts are easy to learn and important to subsequent strategies.

As you work through the multiplication strategy pages, continue to stress the commutative property of multiplication. Students should recognize that if they need to count by groups to solve multiplication problems, it may be more efficient to count by one factor than the other. For example, a problem such as 9×4 (9 groups of 4) is easier to count than 4×9 (4 groups of 9).

Understanding multiplication is enhanced through the exploration of number relationships, the discovery of patterns in and among multiples, and the establishment of personal "anchor facts," most commonly: Times 2, Times 5, and Times 10.

Addition   Here are two ways to use addition to solve multiplication:

Repetitive Addition

Example: $3 \times 8 = ?$

Solution: $8 + 8 + 8 = 24$

Skip Count

Example: $7 \times 5 = ?$

Solution: Count by fives 7 times:
5, 10, 15, 20, 25, 30, 35

Anchor Facts   Use well-known multiplication facts to solve unknowns. The 2s facts, 5s facts, and 10s facts are particularly useful for solving the more difficult Times 7, Times 9, and Times 12 problems.

Times 7 Strategy

Times 7 = Times 5 + Times 2

Example: $7 \times 8 = ?$
Well, I know:
(5×8) and $(2 \times 8) =$
$40 + 16 = 56$

Times 9 Strategy

Times 9 = Times 10 − Times 1

Example: $9 \times 6 = ?$
I do know:
$10 \times 6 = 60$
and $60 − 6 = 54.$

Times 12 Strategy

Times 12 = Times 10 + Times 2

Example: $12 \times 11 = ?$
I can do:
(12×10) and $(12 \times 1) =$
$120 + 12 = 132$

Unknown Facts

$7 \times 6 = ?$ Hmm, I know $6 \times 6 = 36$, so another 6 makes 42.

$4 \times 9 = ?$ I know 2×9 is 18, so double this and I get 36.

$12 \times 13 = ?$ Let's see, $10 \times 13 = 130$ and $2 \times 13 = 26$, so $130 + 26 = 156.$

$19 \times 6 = ?$ Well, $20 \times 6 = 120$ and $120 − 6 = 114.$

Multiplication Strategies

Times 0	0 Times a number is always 0.
Times 1	Times 1 equals the number.
Times 2	Times 2 is double the number.
Times 3	Times 3 is the number tripled. Double the number and add one more group.
Times 4	Times 4 is double Times 2. Times 4 = Times 2 + Times 2. Double the number and double again.
Times 5	Times 5 is like counting nickels. Times 5 is half of Times 10. Times 5 = Times 10 ÷ 2.
Times 6	Times 6 is double Times 3. Times 6 = Times 3 + Times 3. Times 6 = Times 5 + Times 1.
Times 7	Turn Times 7 into smaller multiplication facts: Times 7 = Times 5 + Times 2.
Times 8	Times 8 is double Times 4. Times 8 = Times 4 + Times 4.
Times 9	See Times 9. Think Times 10. Think Times 10 and subtract one group. Times 9 = Times 10 − Times 1.
Times 10	Times 10 increases a number tenfold. Put a 0 in the ones place to increase its value.
Times 11	Single-digit factors Times 11 make double-digit products. (3 × 11 = 33) Times 11 is one group more than Times 10. Times 11 = Times 10 + Times 1.
Times 12	Times 12 = Times 10 + Times 2. Times 12 = Times 6 + Times 6.

Strategy

Counting Equal Groups

Multiplication is totaling items that come in equal groups, equal sets, or equal rows.

Look at the picture and read the problem. Say "times" for the **X** sign.
Complete the number sentence.

3 x 4 means _____3 groups of 4_____.

3 x 3 means _____.

4 x 5 means _____.

Draw:

2 x 12 means _____.

Write a multiplication equation.
Draw a matching picture.

Explain what your equation means.

_____

_____

_____

_____ X _____ = _____   _____

Name _____

Multiplication is commutative. This means the order of the factors does not change the product.

Reverse the factors, and the result is the same.

two groups of 3   equals   three groups of 2

factor   factor
$2 \times 3 = 6$
product

factor   factor
$3 \times 2 = 6$
product

Write the multiplication fact for each picture.
Then draw lines to match the **Turn Around** facts.

2×5

2×6

6×2

5×2

Write the **Turn Around** facts.

$5 \times 4 =$ _20_ $5 \times 2 =$ _10_

$6 \times 3 =$ _18_ $2 \times 7 =$ _14_

Name _____

Strategy

Times 0

Times **0** is always 0.

If you have 0 groups of anything, you have nothing. Nada. Zilcho. Zip.

0 x 6 = _____   0 x 60 = _____   0 x 600 = _____

0 x 7 = _____   0 x 80 = _____   0 x 900 = _____

5 x 0 = _____   50 x 0 = _____   500 x 0 = _____

4 x 0 = _____   30 x 0 = _____   200 x 0 = _____

Strategy

Times 1

Times **1** always equals the number. This is the identity property of multiplication.

Complete the equations.

1 x 9 = _____   1 x 5 = _____   1 x _____ = 4

7 x 1 = _____   17 x 1 = _____   _____ x 1 = 77

Is the missing factor 0 or 1?

6 x ☐ = 0   15 x ☐ = 0   4 x ☐ = 0   8 x ☐ = 8

3 x ☐ = 3   15 x ☐ = 15   7 x ☐ = 0   6 x ☐ = 6

Strategy

Times 2

Times 2 is double the number. Think Doubles facts to solve Times 2.

$2 \times 3 = ?$

Think: two groups of 3

Like this: ▢▢▢ ▢▢▢ · · · · · ·

Which is: $3 + 3 = 6$

Think Doubles facts to solve **Times 2** facts. Complete the chart.

Times 2	Doubles Fact	Answer
2 x 3	3 + 3	6
2 x 4		
2 x 5		
2 x 6		
	7 + 7	
	8 + 8	
		18
		20
2 x 11		
2 x 12		
2 x ____		

Strategy

Times 3

One way to think about **Times 3** is the number tripled.

Use the pictures to help you solve the **Times 3** facts.

Three groups of 2

3 x 2 = _____   2 + 2 + 2

Three groups of 3

3 x 3 = _____   3 + 3 + 3

Three groups of 4

3 x _____ = _____   4 + 4 + 4

Three groups of 5

3 x _____ = _____   5 + 5 + 5

Three groups of 6

3 x _____ = _____   6 + 6 + 6

Strategy

Times 3

Another way to think about **Times 3** is to double the number and add one more group.

$$3 \times 5 = (5 + 5) + 5$$
$$= 10 + 5$$
$$= 15$$

Doubles facts help solve **Times 3** facts.

$$3 \times 7 = (7 + 7) + 7$$
$$= \underline{\hspace{1cm}} + 7$$
$$= \underline{\hspace{1cm}}$$

$$3 \times 8 = (8 + 8) + 8$$
$$= \underline{\hspace{1cm}} + 8$$
$$= \underline{\hspace{1cm}}$$

$$3 \times 9 = (9 + 9) + 9$$
$$= \underline{\hspace{1cm}} + 9$$
$$= \underline{\hspace{1cm}}$$

Strategy

Times 3

Times 3 is the number tripled.
Double the number and
add one more set.

Double the number and add one more set to solve.

$3 \times 12 = (12 + 12) + 12$

$ = \underline{\hspace{1cm}} + 12$

$ = \underline{\hspace{1cm}}$

$3 \times 15 = (15 + 15) + 15$

$ = \underline{\hspace{1cm}} + 15$

$ = \underline{\hspace{1cm}}$

$3 \times 20 = (20 + 20) + 20$

$ = \underline{\hspace{1cm}} + 20$

$ = \underline{\hspace{1cm}}$

Write your own **Times 3** problem.

$3 \times \underline{\hspace{1.5cm}} = (\underline{\hspace{1.5cm}} + \underline{\hspace{1.5cm}}) + \underline{\hspace{1.5cm}}$

$ = \underline{\hspace{1.5cm}} + \underline{\hspace{1.5cm}}$

$ = \underline{\hspace{1.5cm}}$

Building Math Fluency • EMC 3035 • © Evan-Moor Corp.

Name _____

Multiply.

Times 0, 1, 2, 3

0 x 3 = _____   0 x 5 = _____

1 x 3 = _____   1 x 5 = _____

2 x 3 = _____   2 x 5 = _____

3 x 3 = _____   3 x 5 = _____

0 x 4 = _____   0 x 6 = _____

1 x 4 = _____   1 x 6 = _____

2 x 4 = _____   2 x 6 = _____

3 x 4 = _____   3 x 6 = _____

Double Me

2 x 4 = _____   2 x 5 = _____

4 x 2 = _____   5 x 2 = _____

2 x 6 = _____   2 x 9 = _____

6 x 2 = _____   9 x 2 = _____

2 x 10 = _____   2 x 1,000 = _____

2 x 100 = _____   2 x 4,000 = _____

Name _____

Times 2, Times 3

Skip Count up and back by twos.

2, 4, 6, _____, _____, _____, _____, _____, _____, _____

20, 18, 16, _____, _____, _____, _____, _____, _____, _____

Skip Count up and back by threes.

3, 6, 9, _____, _____, _____, _____, _____, _____

30, 27, 24, _____, _____, _____, _____, _____, _____, _____

Complete the chart. Include your own equation and matching picture.

3 x 4 = _____	
3 x _____ = 18	
3 x 3 = _____	
Equation: 3 x _____ = _____	Picture:

Name _____

Times 0 to Times 6 Review

0s Facts

0 x 1 = ____	0 x 6 = ____
0 x 2 = ____	0 x 7 = ____
0 x 3 = ____	0 x 8 = ____
0 x 4 = ____	0 x 9 = ____
0 x 5 = ____	0 x 10 = ____

1s Facts

1 x 1 = ____	1 x 6 = ____
1 x 2 = ____	1 x 7 = ____
1 x 3 = ____	1 x 8 = ____
1 x 4 = ____	1 x 9 = ____
1 x 5 = ____	1 x 10 = ____

2s Facts

2 x 1 = ____	2 x 6 = ____
2 x 2 = ____	2 x 7 = ____
2 x 3 = ____	2 x 8 = ____
2 x 4 = ____	2 x 9 = ____
2 x 5 = ____	2 x 10 = ____

3s Facts

3 x 1 = ____	3 x 6 = ____
3 x 2 = ____	3 x 7 = ____
3 x 3 = ____	3 x 8 = ____
3 x 4 = ____	3 x 9 = ____
3 x 5 = ____	3 x 10 = ____

Skip Count up and back by fours.

4, 8, 12, ____, ____, ____, ____, ____, ____, ____

40, 36, 32, ____, ____, ____, ____, ____, ____, ____

Skip Count up and back by sixes.

6, 12, 18, ____, ____, ____, ____, ____, ____, ____

60, 54, 48, ____, ____, ____, ____, ____, ____, ____

Strategy

Times 10

Times 10 is counting by tens.

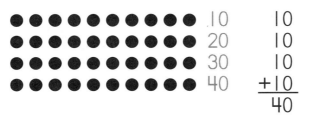

4 x 10 = four groups of 10

	10
20	10
30	10
40	+10
	40

Count by tens.

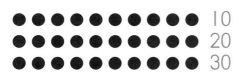

●●●●●●●●●● 10

1 x 10 = ___10___

●●●●●●●●●● 10
●●●●●●●●●● 20

2 x 10 = _____

●●●●●●●●●● 10
●●●●●●●●●● 20
●●●●●●●●●● 30

3 x 10 = _____

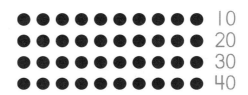

●●●●●●●●●● 10
●●●●●●●●●● 20
●●●●●●●●●● 30
●●●●●●●●●● 40

4 x 10 = _____

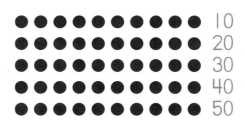

●●●●●●●●●● 10
●●●●●●●●●● 20
●●●●●●●●●● 30
●●●●●●●●●● 40
●●●●●●●●●● 50

5 x 10 = _____

Building Math Fluency • EMC 3035 • © Evan-Moor Corp.

Strategy

Times 10

Times 10 is counting by tens.

Label the rows. Solve the **Times 10** facts.

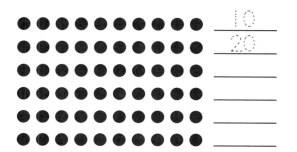

$6 \times 10 =$ _____

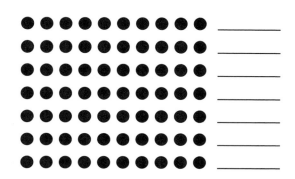

$7 \times 10 =$ _____

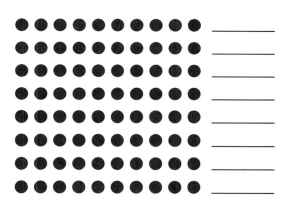

$8 \times 10 =$ _____

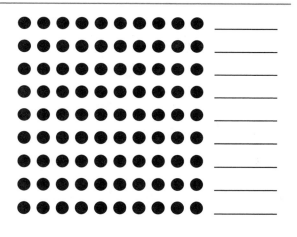

$9 \times 10 =$ _____

Solve.

$10 \times 10 =$ _____   _____ $\times 10 = 130$

$11 \times 10 =$ _____ $14 \times 10 =$ _____

$12 \times 10 =$ _____   _____ $\times 10 = 150$

Name _____

Times 10

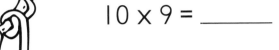

Times 10 is easy. Just put a 0 in the ones place to increase the factor tenfold.

10 x 1 = _____   10 x 9 = _____

10 x 2 = _____   10 x 10 = _____

10 x 3 = _____   10 x 11 = _____

10 x 4 = _____   10 x 12 = _____

10 x 5 = _____   10 x 13 = _____

10 x 6 = _____   10 x 20 = _____

10 x 7 = _____   10 x 30 = _____

10 x 8 = _____   10 x 40 = _____

Write your own **Times 10** equations.

10 x _____ = _____   10 x _____ = _____

Describe what happens to a number when it is multiplied by 10.

_____

--- Word Box ---

digit   ones place   place value   times ten   zero

Strategy

Times 4

Times **4** is the number quadrupled.
Think four sets of the number.

Use the pictures to help you solve the problems.

4 x 2 = _____

2 + 2 + 2 + 2

4 x 3 = _____

3 + 3 + 3 + 3

4 x 4 = _____

4 + 4 + 4 + 4

4 x 5 = _____

5 + 5 + 5 + 5

Remember: **Times 4** is four sets of the number. Solve.

4 x 6 = _____
(6 + 6 + 6 + 6)

4 x 8 = _____
(8 + 8 + 8 + 8)

4 x 7 = _____
(7 + 7 + 7 + 7)

4 x 9 = _____
(9 + 9 + 9 + 9)

Strategy

Times 4

To compute **Times 4**, think 4 sets of the number and then break the sets into 2 groups. It's like **Times 2** + **Times 2**.

4 x 6 = ? Think 4 sets of 6
Then break into 2 groups.

= ___24___

___12___ + ___12___

4 x 7 = ? Think 4 sets of 7
Then break into 2 groups.

= _____

_____ + _____

4 x 8 = ? Think 4 sets of 8
Then break into 2 groups.

= _____

_____ + _____

4 x 9 = ? Think 4 sets of 9
Then break into 2 groups.

= _____

_____ + _____

Strategy

Times 4

Times 4 is double **Times 2**.
Double and double again.

$$4 \times 6 = \overset{\text{double}}{(6 + 6)} + \overset{\text{double}}{(6 + 6)}$$
$$= \text{that's } 12 + 12$$
$$= 24$$

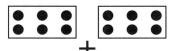  two groups of 6

+

two groups of 6

Solve the problems. Show your work.

$4 \times 5 = (5 + 5) + (5 + 5) = \underline{10 + 10} = $ _____
4 groups of 5

$4 \times 8 = (8 + 8) + (8 + 8) = $ _____
4 groups of 8

$4 \times 9 = (9 + 9) + (9 + 9) = $ _____
4 groups of 9

$4 \times 11 = (11 + 11) + (11 + 11) = $ _____
4 groups of 11

$4 \times 7 = (7 + 7) + (7 + 7) = $ _____
4 groups of 7

Write and solve your own **Times 4** problem.

$4 \times \underline{\quad} = (\underline{\quad} + \underline{\quad}) + (\underline{\quad} + \underline{\quad}) = $ _____
4 groups of ?

Strategy

Times 5

Times 5 is counting groups of five, just like counting nickels.

5   10   15

3 x 5 = _____

4 x 5 = _____

5 x 5 = _____

6 x 5 = _____

Solve. Match the equation with tally marks.

7 x 5 = _____	‖‖‖ ‖‖‖ ‖‖‖ ‖‖‖ ‖‖‖ ‖‖‖ ‖‖‖
8 x 5 = _____	
9 x 5 = _____	
10 x 5 = _____	

Skip Count by fives to solve.

$$\begin{array}{c} 4 \\ \times\ 5 \\ \hline \end{array} \qquad \begin{array}{c} 8 \\ \times\ 5 \\ \hline \end{array} \qquad \begin{array}{c} 6 \\ \times\ 5 \\ \hline \end{array} \qquad \begin{array}{c} 3 \\ \times\ 5 \\ \hline \end{array} \qquad \begin{array}{c} 7 \\ \times\ 5 \\ \hline \end{array} \qquad \begin{array}{c} 5 \\ \times\ 5 \\ \hline \end{array}$$

Strategy

Times 5

Times 5 can be solved by doing **Times 10** and then dividing in half.

Dividing in half is easy if you know the Doubles facts.

3 + 3 = 6, so half of __6__ is __3__

30 + 30 = 60, so half of __60__ is __30__

7 + 7 = 14, so half of __14__ is __7__

70 + 70 = __140__, so half of 140 is _____

To solve **Times 5** problems, think **Times 10** and divide in half.

For 5 x 14, think 10 x 14

10 x 14 = _____

Divide in half.

5 x 14 = _____

For 5 x 16, think 10 x 16

10 x 16 = _____

Divide in half.

5 x 16 = _____

For 5 x 18, think 10 x 18

10 x 18 = _____

Divide in half.

5 x 18 = _____

For 5 x 22, think 10 x 22

10 x 22 = _____

Divide in half.

5 x 22 = _____

Name _____

Times 4, 5, 10

Match.

3 x 4	• 3 groups of 4
4 x 4	• fifteen
3 x 5	• 16
3 x 10	• 5 + 5
2 x 5	• 5 nickels
5 x 5	• 30
7 x 2	• double 7
10 x 6	• 6 + 6 + 6 + 6
6 x 4	• 60

Complete.

	x5	x10
0	0	
1	5	
2	10	
3		
4		
5		
6		
7		
8		
9		
10		

Solve the **Times 4** facts.

4 x 1 = _____   4 x 4 = _____   4 x 7 = _____

4 x 2 = _____   4 x 5 = _____   4 x 8 = _____

4 x 3 = _____   4 x 6 = _____   4 x 9 = _____

Strategy

Times 6

Times 6 is counting by sixes.

Count by sixes to solve. Write numbers to help you.

1 x 6 = ____ ▲▲▲▲▲▲ 6

2 x 6 = ____ ■■■■■■ 6 / 12

3 x 6 = ____ ●●●●●● 6 / 12 / 18

4 x 6 = ____

5 x 6 = ____

6 x 6 = ____

7 x 6 = ____

8 x 6 = ____

9 x 6 = ____

10 x 6 = ____

11 x 6 = ____

12 x 6 = ____

Strategy

Times 6

Times 6 is double **Times 3**.

Times 3 Facts	Double the 3 Facts

$3 \times 4 =$ _____ → Double → $6 \times 4 =$ _____

 Times 3

 Times 3

Times 3

··

Practice **Times 3** and **Times 6**.

$$\begin{array}{cc} 1 & 1 \\ \times\ 3 & \times\ 6 \\ \hline \end{array} \qquad \begin{array}{cc} 2 & 2 \\ \times\ 3 & \times\ 6 \\ \hline \end{array} \qquad \begin{array}{cc} 3 & 3 \\ \times\ 3 & \times\ 6 \\ \hline \end{array}$$

$$\begin{array}{cc} 4 & 4 \\ \times\ 3 & \times\ 6 \\ \hline \end{array} \qquad \begin{array}{cc} 5 & 5 \\ \times\ 3 & \times\ 6 \\ \hline \end{array} \qquad \begin{array}{cc} 6 & 6 \\ \times\ 3 & \times\ 6 \\ \hline \end{array}$$

Strategy

Multiples of 3 and 6

Can you discover how **Times 3** and **Times 6** are related?

Use two colors of crayons.

- Skip Count by threes
  (3, 6, 9, 12...) Shade these
  squares with one color.

- Skip Count by sixes
  (6, 12, 18...) Draw a box
  around these squares with
  a different color.

1	2	3	4	5	6	7	8	9	10
11	12	13	14	15	16	17	18	19	20
21	22	23	24	25	26	27	28	29	30
31	32	33	34	35	36	37	38	39	40
41	42	43	44	45	46	47	48	49	50
51	52	53	54	55	56	57	58	59	60

Complete the table.

	x3	x6
1		
2		
3		
4		
5		
6		
7		
8		
9		
10		

Examine the table. What is the relationship
between **Times 3** and **Times 6**?

_____

_____

_____

Name _____

Times **7** means *groups of seven.*

Add one more 7 each time to solve.

$1 \times 7 =$ _____

$2 \times 7 = 7 + 7 =$ _____

$3 \times 7 = 7 + 7 + 7 =$ _____

$4 \times 7 = 7 + 7 + 7 + 7 =$ _____

$5 \times 7 = 7 + 7 + 7 + 7 + 7 =$ _____

$6 \times 7 = 7 + 7 + 7 + 7 + 7 + 7 =$ _____

$7 \times 7 = 7 + 7 + 7 + 7 + 7 + 7 + 7 =$ _____

$8 \times 7 = 7 + 7 + 7 + 7 + 7 + 7 + 7 + 7 =$ _____

$9 \times 7 = 7 + 7 + 7 + 7 + 7 + 7 + 7 + 7 + 7 =$ _____

$10 \times 7 = 7 + 7 + 7 + 7 + 7 + 7 + 7 + 7 + 7 + 7 =$ _____

$11 \times 7 = 7 + 7 + 7 + 7 + 7 + 7 + 7 + 7 + 7 + 7 + 7 =$ _____

$12 \times 7 = 7 + 7 + 7 + 7 + 7 + 7 + 7 + 7 + 7 + 7 + 7 + 7 =$ _____

Fun Fact

Here's how to remember 7×8:

$$56 = 7 \times 8$$

The digits are in consecutive order.

 Building Math Fluency • EMC 3035 • © Evan-Moor Corp.

Strategy

Times 7

Use multiplication facts that you already know to solve new facts.
Times 7 = Times 5 + Times 2.

$$7 \times 6 = 5 \times 6 \text{ and } 2 \times 6$$

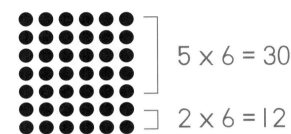

$5 \times 6 = 30$

$2 \times 6 = 12$

$$7 \times 6 = 30 + 12 = 42$$

Solve the problems. Show your work.

$$7 \times 7 = \overset{35}{\overbrace{5 \times 7}} \text{ and } \overset{14}{\overbrace{2 \times 7}} = \underline{\hspace{6cm}}$$

$$7 \times 8 = \overset{40}{\overbrace{5 \times 8}} \text{ and } \overset{16}{\overbrace{2 \times 8}} = \underline{\hspace{6cm}}$$

$$7 \times 6 = 5 \times 6 \text{ and } 2 \times 6 = \underline{\hspace{6cm}}$$

$$7 \times 9 = 5 \times 9 \text{ and } 2 \times 9 = \underline{\hspace{6cm}}$$

$$7 \times 12 = 5 \times 12 \text{ and } 2 \times 12 = \underline{\hspace{6cm}}$$

Name _____

Strategy

Times 8

Times 8 means *groups of eight*.

Add one more 8 each time to solve.

1 x 8 = _____

2 x 8 = _____

3 x 8 = _____

4 x 8 = _____

5 x 8 = _____

6 x 8 = _____

7 x 8 = _____

8 x 8 = _____

9 x 8 = _____

10 x 8 = _____

11 x 8 = _____

12 x 8 = _____

Just for Fun

10 x 8 = _____

20 x 8 = _____
Double 10 x 8

40 x 8 = _____
Double 20 x 8

80 x 8 = _____
Double 40 x 8

Building Math Fluency • EMC 3035 • © Evan-Moor Corp.

Strategy

Times 8

Times 8 is double **Times 4**.

Times 4 Facts

$4 \times 4 =$ _____

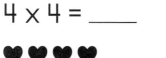

Times 4

Double →

Times 8 Facts

$8 \times 4 =$ _____

Times 4

Times 4

Practice **Times 4** and **Times 8**.

$$\begin{array}{cc} 2 \\ \times\,4 \end{array} \qquad \begin{array}{cc} 2 \\ \times\,8 \end{array} \qquad \begin{array}{cc} 3 \\ \times\,4 \end{array} \qquad \begin{array}{cc} 3 \\ \times\,8 \end{array} \qquad \begin{array}{cc} 4 \\ \times\,4 \end{array} \qquad \begin{array}{cc} 4 \\ \times\,8 \end{array} \qquad \begin{array}{cc} 5 \\ \times\,4 \end{array} \qquad \begin{array}{cc} 5 \\ \times\,8 \end{array}$$

$$\begin{array}{cc} 6 \\ \times\,4 \end{array} \qquad \begin{array}{cc} 6 \\ \times\,8 \end{array} \qquad \begin{array}{cc} 7 \\ \times\,4 \end{array} \qquad \begin{array}{cc} 7 \\ \times\,8 \end{array} \qquad \begin{array}{cc} 8 \\ \times\,4 \end{array} \qquad \begin{array}{cc} 8 \\ \times\,8 \end{array} \qquad \begin{array}{cc} 9 \\ \times\,4 \end{array} \qquad \begin{array}{cc} 9 \\ \times\,8 \end{array}$$

Strategy

Multiples of 2, 4, and 8

Can you discover how **Times 2**, **Times 4**, and **Times 8** are related?

Use three colors of crayons.

- Skip Count by twos (2, 4, 6…) Shade these squares with one color.

- Skip Count by fours (4, 8, 12…) Make an **X** on these squares with a second color.

- Skip Count by eights (8, 16, 24…) Draw a box around these squares with a third color.

1	2	3	4	5	6	7	8	9	10
11	12	13	14	15	16	17	18	19	20
21	22	23	24	25	26	27	28	29	30
31	32	33	34	35	36	37	38	39	40
41	42	43	44	45	46	47	48	49	50
51	52	53	54	55	56	57	58	59	60
61	62	63	64	65	66	67	68	69	70
71	72	73	74	75	76	77	78	79	80

Complete the table.

	x2	x4	x8
1			
2			
3			
4			
5			
6			
7			
8			
9			
10			

Examine the table.
Explain what you notice.

_____

_____

_____

Name _____

Times 6, 7, 8

Complete the chart.

Words	Factors	Product
three sets of six	3 x 6	18
five sets of seven	5 x 7	
five sets of eight		
four sets of seven	4 x 7	
	3 x 8	
	6 x 6	36

Show how to solve **6 x 8**.
Use words, numbers, and/or pictures.

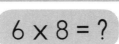

6 x 8 = ?

Strategy

Times 9

Times **9** means *groups of nine.*

Add one more 9 each time to solve.

9s Facts	Product
1 x 9	9
2 x 9	18
3 x 9	
4 x 9	
5 x 9	
6 x 9	
7 x 9	
8 x 9	
9 x 9	
10 x 9	

Study the products listed above.
What patterns can you find?

_____

_____

Solve.

$11 \times 9 =$ _____ $12 \times 9 =$ _____ $13 \times 9 =$ _____

Strategy

Times 9

See Times 9. Think Times 10.
Instead of groups of nine, think **Times 10** and subtract one group.
Times 9 = Times 10 − Times 1.

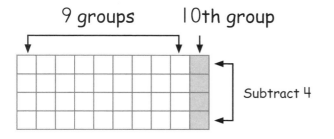

4 × 9 = ?

For 4 × 9, do 4 × 10.
Then subtract 4.

9 groups   10th group

Subtract 4

4 × 10 = 40
4 × 9 = 40 − 4 = 36

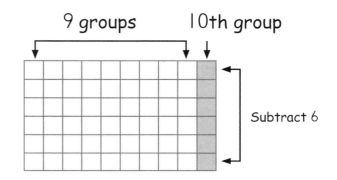

6 × 9 = ?

For 6 × 9, do 6 × 10.
Then subtract 6.

9 groups   10th group

Subtract 6

6 × 10 = 60
6 × 9 = 60 − 6 = 54

Use **Times 9** to solve these problems.

3 × 9 = ?

Think **Times 10**.
Then subtract **Times 1**.

3 × 9 = (3 × 10) − 3 = ____

7 × 9 = ?

Think **Times 10**.
Then subtract **Times 1**.

7 × 9 = (7 × 10) − 7 = ____

Solve these on your own.

8 × 9 = (__8__ × 10) − __8__ = ____

9 × 9 = (__9__ × 10) − __9__ = ____

12 × 9 = (__12__ × 10) − __12__ = ____

Strategy

Times 9

Ways to compute Times 9:
- Anchor Facts
- See 9. Think 10.

Anchor Facts

Build on facts you know, like **Times 2** and **Times 5**, to figure other facts.

Example: For 6×9, think **Times 5**.
You know $5 \times 9 = 45$,
so 6×9 is $45 + 9 = 54$.

See 9. Think 10.

Multiply by 10, then subtract.

$$6 \times 9 = (6 \times 10) - 6$$
$$= 60 - 6 = 54$$

Solve the problems.
Use **Anchor Facts** or **See 9**. **Think 10**.
Show your work.

I know that
$9 + 9 = 18$,
so four 9s is
$18 + 18 = 36$.

$$\begin{array}{r} 4 \\ \times\ 9 \\ \hline 36 \end{array}$$

$$\begin{array}{r} 9 \\ \times\ 2 \\ \hline \end{array}$$

$$\begin{array}{r} 6 \\ \times\ 9 \\ \hline \end{array}$$

$$\begin{array}{r} 7 \\ \times\ 9 \\ \hline \end{array}$$

$$\begin{array}{r} 9 \\ \times\ 3 \\ \hline \end{array}$$

$$\begin{array}{r} 9 \\ \times\ 7 \\ \hline \end{array}$$

$$\begin{array}{r} 5 \\ \times\ 9 \\ \hline \end{array}$$

$$\begin{array}{r} 9 \\ \times\ 8 \\ \hline \end{array}$$

$$\begin{array}{r} 9 \\ \times\ 3 \\ \hline \end{array}$$

Building Math Fluency • EMC 3035 • © Evan-Moor Corp.

Name _____

Discover the pattern for **Times 11** with single-digit factors.

Find the product.

$3 \times 11 =$ _____

$5 \times 11 =$ _____

$7 \times 11 =$ _____

$8 \times 11 =$ _____

Do you notice what I notice with **Times 11** facts?

$$\begin{array}{r} 11 \\ \times\ 6 \\ \hline \end{array}$$
$$\begin{array}{r} 11 \\ \times\ 4 \\ \hline \end{array}$$
$$\begin{array}{r} 11 \\ \times\ 9 \\ \hline \end{array}$$
$$\begin{array}{r} 11 \\ \times\ 2 \\ \hline \end{array}$$

To do **Times 11** with double-digit factors, multiply by 10 and add one more group.

$11 \times 11 = (11 \times 10) + 11 =$ _121_

$12 \times 11 = (12 \times 10) + 12 =$ _____

$15 \times 11 = (15 \times 10) + 15 =$ _____

$17 \times 11 = (17 \times 10) + 17 =$ _____

_____ $\times 11 = ($ ___ $\times$ ___ $) +$ ___ $=$ _____

Times 11 is **Times 10** and one more group.

Strategy

Times 12

1 Add sets of 12

12 + 12 + 12   12 + 12 + 12 + 12 + 12

3 x 12 = _____   5 x 12 = _____

2 **Times 12** is double **Times 6**.

2 x 12 = (2 x 6) + (2 x 6) = _____ + _____ = _____

4 x 12 = (4 x 6) + (4 x 6) = _____ + _____ = _____

3 **Times 12** is **Times 10** and **Times 2**.
Multiply by 10 and add two more groups.

$\overbrace{}^{70}$ $\overbrace{}^{14}$

7 x 12 = (7 x 10) + 7 + 7 = _____

8 x 12 = (8 x 10) + 8 + 8 = _____

9 x 12 = (9 x 10) + 9 + 9 = _____

Name _____

Times 9, 11, 12

11s Facts	
11 x 1 = ___	11 x 6 = ___
11 x 2 = ___	11 x 7 = ___
11 x 3 = ___	11 x 8 = ___
11 x 4 = ___	11 x 9 = ___
11 x 5 = ___	11 x 10 = ___

12s Facts	
12 x 1 = ___	12 x 6 = ___
12 x 2 = ___	12 x 7 = ___
12 x 3 = ___	12 x 8 = ___
12 x 4 = ___	12 x 9 = ___
12 x 5 = ___	12 x 10 = ___

Match and solve.

10 + 10 + 10 + 10 + 10

7 dozen

Eleven buses each
hold 10 passengers

12 dimes

forty-four

- 7 x 12 = _____

- 5 x 10 = _____

- 12 x 10 = _____

- 4 x 11 = _____

- 11 x 10 = _____

Knowing 10s facts can help you solve related facts like 9s, 11s, and 12s.
Explain and give an example.

_____

_____

Name _____

Square Numbers

When both factors are the same, the product is a **square number**.
Square numbers have equal rows and columns.

Complete the two-page chart.

Picture	Factors	Square Number
●	1 × 1	1
●● ●●	2 × 2	4
●●● ●●● ●●●	3 × 3	9
●●●● (4×4)		
●●●●● (5×5)		
●●●●●● (6×6)		
●●●●●●● (7×7)		

Building Math Fluency • EMC 3035 • © Evan-Moor Corp.

Name

Square Numbers (continued)

Picture	Factors	Square Number

Complete the list of square numbers.

1, 4, _____, _____, _____, _____, _____, _____, _____, 100

Examine your list for patterns, and record what you notice.

_____

_____

 **Mixed Strategies Practice**

Multiplication Table

Record the products.

x	1	2	3	4	5	6	7	8	9	10
1										
2										
3										
4										
5										
6										
7										
8										
9										
10										

Color the boxes.

▶ When both factors are the same, the product is called a **square number**. Color the square numbers red.

▶ Multiples of five end in the numbers: _____ and _____ Color multiples of 5 blue.

Talk about it.

▶ Which product or products occur most frequently in your table?

▶ Are there more odd products or even products in your table? Why?

 Building Math Fluency • EMC 3035 • © Evan-Moor Corp.

Teaching Division Strategies

Pages 89–101 present practice with division strategies that are introductory in nature and that are presented primarily as a means to reinforce multiplication concepts. These strategies focus on key number patterns and number relationships to promote fact mastery and build computational fluency.

To divide means to share items equally; to separate quantities into "fair shares."

$$\overset{\text{dividend}}{\underset{}{16}} \div \overset{\text{divisor}}{\underset{}{8}} = \underset{\text{quotient}}{2}$$

Basic Properties of Division

0 divided by a number is 0.

$0 \div N = 0$

A number divided by itself is 1.

$N \div N = 1$

A number divided by 1 equals the number.

$N \div 1 = N$

Note: **N ÷ 0** can not be done. If **N ÷ 0 = A** was possible, then it would follow that **A × 0 = N**, but this is <u>not</u> true. Another way to view this is that you can't divide a quantity into groups of 0.

Division Strategies

Use Doubles Facts

$12 \div 2 = 6$ because two sixes make 12.

$18 \div 2 = 9$ because two nines make 18.

Think Multiplication

24 ÷ 6 = ?

Think: 6 × *what* = 24. The answer is 4.

$24 \div 6 = 4$

54 ÷ 9 = ?

Think: 9 × *what* = 54. The answer is 6.

$54 \div 9 = 6$

Division Strategies

Division of 0	0 divided by any number is 0. $0 \div 6 = 0$ If there are 0 things, there is nothing to divide into groups.
	Division by 0 is **not** possible. $8 \div 0 =$ You can't divide 8 things into 0 groups. That makes no sense.
A Number Divided by Itself	A number divided by itself is 1. $3 \div 3 = 1 \qquad 89 \div 89 = 1$
Division by 1	A number divided by 1 equals the number. $3 \div 1 = 3 \qquad 89 \div 1 = 89$
Division by 2	A number divided by 2 is half the number. Use Doubles facts to solve Division by 2. $8 \div 2 = ?$
Division by 3–12	Use related multiplication to solve division problems. For example: $40 \div 5 = ?$ Think: $5 \times$ *what* $= 40$ $5 \times 8 = 40,$ so $40 \div 5 = 8.$

Building Math Fluency • EMC 3035 • © Evan-Moor Corp.

Strategy

Making Equal Groups

When you divide, you separate items into equal groups.

10 ÷ 2 means:
10 divided into 2 equal groups.

10 ÷ 2 = 5

9 ÷ 3 means:
9 divided into 3 equal groups.

16 ÷ 4 means:
16 divided into 4 equal groups.

Complete the sentence.
Draw a picture to match.

12 ÷ 3 means:

_____

_____

_____

Strategy

Division of 0

Division of 0 is always 0.
If there are 0 items, there is
nothing to divide into groups.

Divide.

$0 \div 6 =$ _____ $0 \div 3 =$ _____ $0 \div 5 =$ _____

$0 \div 7 =$ _____ $0 \div 84 =$ _____ $0 \div$ _____ = _____

Division of 0 is not possible. **5 ÷ 0** can't be done.

How could you divide 5 items into 0 groups? It makes no sense.

Strategy

Division by 1

A number divided by 1
equals the number.

   If there are 3 bananas and 1 monkey,
the monkey gets 3 bananas.
$$3 \div 1 = 3$$

   If there are 6 bananas and 1 monkey,
the monkey gets 6 bananas.
$$6 \div 1 = 6$$

Divide.

$7 \div 1 =$ _____ $9 \div 1 =$ _____   _____ $\div 1 = 4$

$5 \div 1 =$ _____ $15 \div 1 =$ _____   _____ $\div 1 = 8$

Strategy
A Number Divided by Itself

A number divided by itself equals 1.

Let's think about monkeys.
Imagine 4 monkeys and 4 bananas.
If you divide the bananas equally,
each monkey will get 1 banana.

$$4 \div 4 = 1$$

Divide.

$7 \div 7 =$ _____ $3 \div 3 =$ _____ $6 \div 6 =$ _____

$5 \div 5 =$ _____ $9 \div 9 =$ _____   _____ $\div$ _____ $= 1$

$14 \div 14 =$ _____ $20 \div 20 =$ _____ $8 \div 8 =$ _____

Review

Match.

$10 \div 1$ • 10 divided into 5 groups

$0 \div 10$ • zero

$10 \div 5$ • ten

$10 \div 10$ • one

Strategy

Division by 2

Division by 2 means to divide an amount into two equal sets. Divide the quantity in half. Think **Doubles**.

Divide in half!

$4 \div 2 = 2$

Divide. Draw dots to help you.

$6 \div 2 = \underline{}$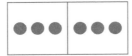

$10 \div 2 = \underline{}$

$8 \div 2 = \underline{}$

$14 \div 2 = \underline{}$

$20 \div 2 = \underline{}$

$16 \div 2 = \underline{}$

$18 \div 2 = \underline{}$

$\underline{} \div 2 = 6$

$\underline{} \div 2 = 11$

$\underline{} \div 2 = 12$

Strategy

Division by 3

When you divide by 3, you are distributing items into three equal groups.

Imagine you are playing cards with two friends. All three of you need the same number of cards. The game has 18 cards. You deal them out one at a time.

Three Equal Groups

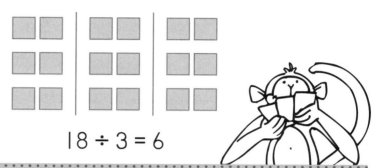

$18 \div 3 = 6$

Use tally marks to make three equal groups. Complete the equation.

$12 \div 3 =$ _____ | |||| | |||| | |||| |

$15 \div 3 =$ _____

$18 \div 3 =$ _____

$24 \div 3 =$ _____

$27 \div 3 =$ _____

$30 \div 3 =$ _____

Division   **93**

Strategy

Division by 2 and 3

Division is related to multiplication. You can solve division problems by thinking of multiplication facts.

$12 \div 2 = 6$
12 divided into 2 groups is 6.

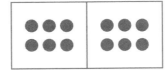

$2 \times 6 = 12$
2 groups of 6 is 12.

Draw dots to help you complete the related equations.

Division   **Multiplication**

$15 \div 3 = 5$ $3 \times \underline{} = 15$

$21 \div 3 = 7$ $3 \times \underline{} = 21$

$27 \div 3 = \underline{}$ $3 \times \underline{} = 27$

$16 \div 2 = \underline{}$ $2 \times \underline{} = 16$

$18 \div 2 = \underline{}$ $2 \times \underline{} = 18$

$18 \div 3 = \underline{}$ $3 \times \underline{} = 18$

Strategy

Division by 4 and 5

When you divide, it helps to think of the related multiplication fact.

A Fact Family

The numbers 4, 5, and 20 make four related equations:

$4 \times 5 = 20$ $20 \div 4 = 5$

$5 \times 4 = 20$ $20 \div 5 = 4$

Solve. Think about the related multiplication fact.

$4 \times ? = 24$

$24 \div 4 = $ _____

$4 \times ? = 32$

$32 \div 4 = $ _____

$4 \times ? = 36$

$36 \div 4 = $ _____

$4 \times ? = 28$

$28 \div 4 = $ _____

$5 \times ? = 25$

$25 \div 5 = $ _____

$5 \times ? = 45$

$45 \div 5 = $ _____

$30 \div 5 = $ _____

$40 \div 5 = $ _____

$55 \div 5 = $ _____

$35 \div 5 = $ _____

Name _____

Fill in the **Times 6** multiplication chart.

x	1	2	3	4	5	6	7	8	9	10	11	12
6	6	12	18									

Use the chart to help you solve the division problems.

$60 \div 6 =$ __10__ $30 \div 6 =$ _____ $12 \div 6 =$ _____

$24 \div 6 =$ _____ $66 \div 6 =$ _____ $54 \div 6 =$ _____

$36 \div 6 =$ _____ $48 \div 6 =$ _____ $72 \div 6 =$ _____

Fill in the **Times 7** multiplication chart.

x	1	2	3	4	5	6	7	8	9	10	11	12
7	7	14										

Use the chart to help you solve the division problems.

$77 \div 7 =$ _____ $70 \div 7 =$ _____ $63 \div 7 =$ _____

$14 \div 7 =$ _____ $84 \div 7 =$ _____ $21 \div 7 =$ _____

$28 \div 7 =$ _____ $56 \div 7 =$ _____ $35 \div 7 =$ _____

$42 \div 7 =$ _____ $49 \div 7 =$ _____ $7 \div 7 =$ _____

Strategy

Division by 8 and 9

To divide, think multiplication.

Fill in the multiplication chart.
Use it to find each quotient.

x	8	9
1	8	9
2	16	18
3	24	
4		
5		
6		
7		
8		
9		
10		
11		
12		

$88 \div 8 =$ _____

$48 \div 8 =$ _____

$90 \div 9 =$ _____

$27 \div 9 =$ _____

$56 \div 8 =$ _____

$40 \div 8 =$ _____

$32 \div 8 =$ _____

$96 \div 8 =$ _____

$9 \div 9 =$ _____

$16 \div 8 =$ _____

$36 \div 9 =$ _____

$64 \div 8 =$ _____

$45 \div 9 =$ _____

$54 \div 9 =$ _____

$81 \div 9 =$ _____

$24 \div 8 =$ _____

$63 \div 9 =$ _____

$72 \div 9 =$ _____

Strategy

Division by 10 and 11

Think multiplication to divide.

Solve and match the related facts.

11 × 5 = __55__

10 × 8 = _____

11 × 9 = _____

11 × 1 = _____

10 × 7 = _____

10 × 4 = _____

0 × 11 = _____

● 99 ÷ 11 = _____

● 55 ÷ 11 = __5__

● 80 ÷ 10 = _____

● 11 ÷ 11 = _____

● 70 ÷ 10 = _____

● 0 ÷ 11 = _____

● 40 ÷ 10 = _____

Building Math Fluency • EMC 3035 • © Evan-Moor Corp.

Strategy

Division by 12

Think multiplication to divide.

Fill in the multiplication chart.
Use it to find each quotient.

x	1	2	3	4	5	6	7	8	9	10	11	12
12	12	24										

$24 \div 12 = $ _____ $48 \div 12 = $ _____ $108 \div 12 = $ _____

$36 \div 12 = $ _____ $60 \div 12 = $ _____ $132 \div 12 = $ _____

$96 \div 12 = $ _____ $72 \div 12 = $ _____ $144 \div 12 = $ _____

Review

$80 \div 10 = $ _____ $72 \div 9 = $ _____ $64 \div 8 = $ _____

$77 \div 11 = $ _____ $56 \div 8 = $ _____ $28 \div 4 = $ _____

$36 \div 6 = $ _____ $54 \div 9 = $ _____ $48 \div 8 = $ _____

$35 \div 7 = $ _____ $25 \div 5 = $ _____ $45 \div 9 = $ _____

Strategy

Division with Remainders

Think of the nearest multiplication fact.

Imagine 3 monkeys have 10 bananas.
That's 3 bananas for each monkey plus one extra.

$$3 + 3 + 3 + 1 = 10$$

Each monkey gets 3 bananas and 1 is left over.
That's $(3 \times 3) + 1 = 10$

The extra items are called **remainders**.
They are notated by an **R**.

$$10 \div 3 = 3 \text{ R}1$$

Find each quotient and remainder.

$16 \div 5 =$ _3 R1_ $13 \div 3 =$ _____ $14 \div 3 =$ _____

$17 \div 8 =$ _2 R1_ $11 \div 2 =$ _____ $9 \div 4 =$ _____

$10 \div 4 =$ _____ $10 \div 3 =$ _____ $13 \div 4 =$ _____

$11 \div 5 =$ _____ $13 \div 6 =$ _____ $15 \div 7 =$ _____

Building Math Fluency • EMC 3035 • © Evan-Moor Corp.

Strategy

Division with Remainders

Think of the nearest multiplication fact.

Problem	My Solution Steps

22 ÷ 7 = ?	I have 22 items to divide into 7 groups. What Times 7 is close to 22?
	
	  2 x 7 is 14. That's not close enough to 22.
	  4 x 7 is 28. That's over 22.
	  3 x 7 is 21. That's just one away from 22.
	
	I can divide my 22 items into 3 groups of 7 and have 1 remaining.
	
	22 ÷ 7 = 3 R1

Divide.

Problem	My Solution Steps
23 ÷ 5 = ?	Explain your solution.
28 ÷ 9 = ?	Explain your solution.

How to Use
Test Your Skills

The *Test Your Skills* exercises on pages 103–132 provide multiple opportunities for assessment of computational skills. Each test series—for addition, subtraction, multiplication, and division—begins with easier problems and increases in difficulty.

Each page in the *Test Your Skills* section may be used multiple times and in different ways to build computational skills and improve fact fluency.

Mixed Strategies Practice

The tests provide the opportunity to practice many of the computational strategies presented in this book. For each problem, students should ask themselves: Which strategy best suits the numbers involved?

Strategy Focus

Have students select one strategy at a time to practice. They examine the problems and then circle and solve those that fit the focus strategy.

Assessment

Use the tests to determine how students are progressing in their acquisition of number facts. If appropriate, allow students to set their own goals for improvement of computation speed.

Student Self-Evaluation

The record area at the bottom of each *Test Your Skills* page affords students the opportunity to assess their own performance and use of computational strategies. This self-evaluation is an important part of the skill-building process.

After completing a *Test Your Skills* page, allow time for students to share the various strategies they used.

Name _____   My Score _____

Test Your Skills

0 + 0	5 + 1	7 + 2	4 + 3	6 + 4	2 + 0
5 + 5	0 + 8	7 + 1	3 + 2	1 + 1	10 + 0
6 + 1	4 + 0	5 + 2	7 + 3	4 + 4	8 + 1
3 + 3	5 + 4	2 + 7	2 + 3	4 + 1	5 + 3
4 + 2	6 + 3	8 + 2	4 + 5	6 + 2	9 + 1
2 + 8	4 + 6	3 + 4	2 + 5	2 + 2	3 + 5

How am I doing?

Accuracy

❏ I got them all right!
❏ I missed a couple.
❏ I will practice these:
(List up to 5 facts.)

Efficiency

I used these strategies:

❏ Count Up
❏ Doubles
❏ Tens Partners
❏ Other

Time

I finished in:

_____

My next goal is:

_____

Name _____   My Score _____

Test Your Skills

10 + 1	6 + 5	9 + 6	14 + 1	8 + 3	6 + 7
8 + 5	9 + 2	8 + 7	6 + 6	12 + 0	9 + 6
11 + 2	8 + 6	10 + 3	7 + 4	3 + 9	12 + 1
7 + 6	13 + 2	8 + 5	13 + 1	7 + 8	9 + 4
6 + 9	7 + 7	9 + 3	5 + 8	12 + 2	11 + 4
9 + 5	8 + 4	15 + 0	4 + 9	7 + 5	3 + 8

How am I doing?

Accuracy

❏ I got them all right!
❏ I missed a couple.
❏ I will practice these:
(List up to 5 facts.)

Efficiency

I used these strategies:

❏ Count Up
❏ Doubles
❏ Doubles Plus 1
❏ Plus 8, 9, 10

Time

I finished in:

_____

My next goal is:

_____

Building Math Fluency • EMC 3035 • © Evan-Moor Corp.

Name _____ My Score _____

Test Your Skills

10 + 5	9 + 3	6 + 6	11 + 1	7 + 5	2 + 9
5 + 9	7 + 4	12 + 3	9 + 5	8 + 6	4 + 8
11 + 0	6 + 8	7 + 6	8 + 4	5 + 7	6 + 9
9 + 4	14 + 0	8 + 7	9 + 6	6 + 5	8 + 6
14 + 1	9 + 2	10 + 4	8 + 5	11 + 3	4 + 7
5 + 6	8 + 3	7 + 8	10 + 2	9 + 5	9 + 6

How am I doing?

Accuracy
❏ I got them all right!
❏ I missed a couple.
❏ I will practice these:
(List up to 5 facts.)

Efficiency
I used these strategies:
❏ Count Up
❏ Doubles
❏ Doubles Plus 1
❏ Plus 8, 9, 10

Time
I finished in:

_____

My next goal is:

_____

Name _____ My Score _____

Test Your Skills

18 + 1	9 + 7	11 + 5	14 + 3	13 + 6	10 + 9
12 + 7	16 + 0	10 + 10	13 + 4	11 + 8	14 + 6
15 + 4	11 + 9	17 + 2	9 + 8	12 + 5	16 + 3
16 + 2	12 + 4	11 + 6	19 + 1	9 + 9	13 + 7
12 + 6	20 + 0	14 + 4	7 + 9	15 + 5	8 + 8
17 + 3	12 + 8	13 + 5	8 + 9	18 + 2	16 + 4

How am I doing?

Accuracy
❏ I got them all right!
❏ I missed a couple.
❏ I will practice these:
(List up to 5 facts.)

Efficiency
I used these strategies:
❏ Doubles
❏ Doubles Plus 1 or 2
❏ Tens Partners
❏ Plus 8, 9, 10

Time
I finished in:
_____
My next goal is:
_____

Name _____   My Score _____

Test Your Skills

18 + 2	9 + 4	6 + 6	8 + 5	16 + 3	7 + 5
8 + 6	7 + 3	5 + 5	9 + 8	6 + 2	10 + 5
7 + 4	15 + 5	9 + 0	6 + 5	8 + 7	4 + 4
9 + 2	7 + 6	8 + 4	5 + 4	9 + 3	5 + 2
17 + 3	7 + 1	9 + 5	6 + 3	8 + 8	9 + 7
9 + 9	6 + 4	8 + 3	9 + 6	19 + 1	7 + 7

How am I doing?

Accuracy
❑ I got them all right!
❑ I missed a couple.
❑ I will practice these:
(List up to 5 facts.)

Efficiency
I used these strategies:
❑ Count Up
❑ Doubles Plus 1 or 2
❑ Tens Partners
❑ Plus 8, 9, 10

Time
I finished in:
_____

My next goal is:
_____

Name _____ My Score _____

Test Your Skills

2 − 0	7 − 4	9 − 7	10 − 9	6 − 3	2 − 1
4 − 2	8 − 5	8 − 8	10 − 8	6 − 1	10 − 1
8 − 2	10 − 3	6 − 4	9 − 5	7 − 2	8 − 6
6 − 5	9 − 2	8 − 3	10 − 6	9 − 4	7 − 3
7 − 5	10 − 5	5 − 2	8 − 4	7 − 1	9 − 6
6 − 2	5 − 3	8 − 7	9 − 3	10 − 4	9 − 8

How am I doing?

Accuracy
❏ I got them all right!
❏ I missed a couple.
❏ I will practice these:
(List up to 5 facts.)

Efficiency
I used these strategies:
❏ Count Back 1, 2, or 3
❏ Count Up from bottom number
❏ Doubles Subtraction
❏ Tens Partners Subtraction

Time
I finished in:

_____

My next goal is:

_____

Building Math Fluency • EMC 3035 • © Evan-Moor Corp.

Name _____   My Score _____

Test Your Skills

11 − 5	13 − 7	12 − 4	14 − 8	11 − 9	15 − 3
14 − 6	12 − 7	11 − 2	13 − 5	12 − 6	14 − 7
12 − 5	15 − 0	15 − 9	13 − 9	12 − 3	12 − 9
14 − 5	13 − 6	11 − 4	12 − 8	15 − 6	12 − 10
11 − 3	15 − 7	13 − 1	11 − 6	13 − 8	15 − 5
13 − 4	11 − 7	14 − 9	15 − 8	11 − 8	15 − 10

How am I doing?

Accuracy
❏ I got them all right!
❏ I missed a couple.
❏ I will practice these:
(List up to 5 facts.)

Efficiency
I used these strategies:
❏ Count Back 1, 2, or 3
❏ Count Up from bottom number
❏ Doubles Subtraction
❏ Minus 10, 9, 8

Time
I finished in:
_____
My next goal is:
_____

Name _____   My Score _____

Test Your Skills

15 − 10	13 − 8	11 − 8	15 − 5	11 − 5	14 − 6
13 − 7	12 − 7	15 − 9	11 − 4	12 − 8	13 − 9
11 − 3	15 − 7	11 − 7	13 − 4	11 − 9	12 − 6
12 − 3	13 − 1	15 − 6	12 − 9	14 − 7	15 − 0
12 − 10	13 − 5	14 − 9	15 − 3	13 − 6	15 − 8
14 − 8	12 − 4	11 − 2	12 − 5	14 − 5	11 − 6

How am I doing?

Accuracy
❑ I got them all right!
❑ I missed a couple.
❑ I will practice these:
(List up to 5 facts.)

Efficiency
I used these strategies:
❑ Count Back 1, 2, or 3
❑ Count Up from bottom number
❑ Think Addition
❑ Other

Time
I finished in:

_____

My next goal is:

Name _____   My Score _____

Test Your Skills

| 17 | 20 | 16 | 18 | 20 | 16 |
| - 2 | - 10 | - 9 | - 9 | - 8 | - 0 |

| 20 | 16 | 19 | 17 | 20 | 16 |
| - 5 | - 8 | - 0 | - 6 | - 15 | - 6 |

| 19 | 17 | 20 | 16 | 17 | 20 |
| - 5 | - 3 | - 18 | - 9 | - 14 | - 7 |

| 20 | 18 | 17 | 19 | 20 | 18 |
| - 1 | - 8 | - 8 | - 6 | - 3 | - 5 |

| 17 | 16 | 16 | 20 | 17 | 18 |
| - 10 | - 7 | - 2 | - 4 | - 9 | - 7 |

| 18 | 17 | 20 | 16 | 19 | 20 |
| - 6 | - 8 | - 9 | - 7 | - 4 | - 20 |

How am I doing?

Accuracy

❏ I got them all right!
❏ I missed a couple.
❏ I will practice these:
(List up to 5 facts.)

Efficiency

I used these strategies:

❏ Count Back 1, 2, or 3
❏ Count Up from bottom number
❏ Think Addition
❏ Other

Time

I finished in:

_____

My next goal is:

_____

Name _____   My Score _____

Test Your Skills

20 − 10	9 − 5	12 − 7	13 − 5	11 − 9	14 − 7

10 − 6	11 − 5	16 − 1	15 − 6	16 − 7	13 − 8

14 − 5	16 − 9	8 − 3	12 − 9	17 − 9	15 − 8

13 − 6	20 − 15	12 − 6	14 − 8	18 − 9	11 − 6

15 − 7	14 − 6	13 − 9	9 − 6	16 − 8	12 − 8

11 − 7	9 − 7	15 − 9	17 − 8	13 − 7	14 − 9

How am I doing?

Accuracy
❏ I got them all right!
❏ I missed a couple.
❏ I will practice these:
(List up to 5 facts.)

Efficiency
I used these strategies:
❏ Count Up from bottom number
❏ Doubles Subtraction
❏ Think Addition
❏ Other

Time
I finished in:

_____

My next goal is:

_____

Name _____   My Score _____

Test Your Skills

2 × 2	10 × 0	1 × 3	1 × 1	4 × 2	1 × 9
8 × 1	9 × 0	0 × 7	4 × 1	3 × 1	1 × 10
2 × 5	3 × 0	1 × 2	2 × 3	10 × 1	11 × 0
2 × 1	1 × 6	3 × 3	6 × 0	1 × 5	12 × 0
1 × 0	3 × 2	5 × 2	1 × 8	9 × 1	5 × 1
7 × 1	2 × 4	4 × 1	2 × 0	6 × 1	8 × 0

How am I doing?

Accuracy

❏ I got them all right!
❏ I missed a couple.
❏ I will practice these:
(List up to 5 facts.)

Efficiency

I used these strategies:

❏ Times 0
❏ Times 1
❏ Doubles Facts
❏ Skip Count

Time

I finished in:

_____

My next goal is:

_____

Name _____   My Score _____

Test Your Skills

2 × 6	5 × 3	4 × 6	7 × 2	3 × 7	12 × 2
10 × 2	3 × 4	11 × 1	2 × 9	6 × 4	11 × 2
12 × 1	6 × 2	5 × 4	7 × 3	4 × 3	6 × 3
4 × 5	3 × 8	2 × 7	3 × 5	8 × 2	3 × 6
2 × 8	9 × 2	12 × 1	4 × 4	10 × 2	12 × 2
6 × 4	11 × 2	5 × 5	3 × 8	11 × 1	8 × 3

How am I doing?

Accuracy
❏ I got them all right!
❏ I missed a couple.
❏ I will practice these:
(List up to 5 facts.)

Efficiency
I used these strategies:
❏ Times 1
❏ Doubles Facts
❏ Doubles Times 2
❏ Skip Count

Time
I finished in:
_____
My next goal is:
_____

Name _____   My Score _____

Test Your Skills

6 x 4	2 x 8	11 x 2	2 x 7	8 x 3	12 x 1
12 x 2	3 x 8	10 x 2	5 x 5	4 x 6	3 x 5
11 x 1	9 x 2	2 x 6	4 x 4	8 x 2	5 x 4
3 x 4	6 x 3	12 x 2	7 x 2	4 x 5	3 x 6
5 x 3	11 x 2	2 x 9	3 x 7	12 x 1	11 x 1
6 x 2	10 x 2	7 x 3	6 x 4	4 x 3	3 x 8

How am I doing?

Accuracy
❏ I got them all right!
❏ I missed a couple.
❏ I will practice these:
(List up to 5 facts.)

Efficiency
I used these strategies:
❏ Times 1
❏ Doubles Facts
❏ Doubles Times 2
❏ Skip Count

Time
I finished in:

_____

My next goal is:

_____

Name _____   My Score _____

Test Your Skills

4 x 7	6 x 5	5 x 9	6 x 7	10 x 3	8 x 4
7 x 4	12 x 3	11 x 4	4 x 9	5 x 7	9 x 3
10 x 5	8 x 6	5 x 6	7 x 7	12 x 4	11 x 3
9 x 3	7 x 5	4 x 8	9 x 4	10 x 3	6 x 8
6 x 6	10 x 4	7 x 6	12 x 3	10 x 5	11 x 4
9 x 5	5 x 8	3 x 9	8 x 5	12 x 4	10 x 4

How am I doing?

Accuracy
❏ I got them all right!
❏ I missed a couple.
❏ I will practice these:
(List up to 5 facts.)

Efficiency
I used these strategies:
❏ Build on known facts
   of x2, x5, x10
❏ Double x3, x4, x6
❏ Other

Time
I finished in:

_____

My next goal is:

Building Math Fluency • EMC 3035 • © Evan-Moor Corp.

Name _____   My Score _____

Test Your Skills

6 × 6	11 × 4	7 × 5	3 × 9	10 × 3	7 × 6
10 × 5	12 × 4	4 × 8	10 × 4	9 × 5	12 × 3
9 × 4	11 × 3	5 × 8	9 × 3	6 × 8	8 × 4
7 × 4	10 × 3	4 × 7	5 × 6	5 × 9	11 × 4
6 × 5	7 × 7	4 × 9	12 × 3	10 × 4	12 × 4
8 × 5	10 × 5	6 × 7	5 × 7	11 × 3	8 × 6

How am I doing?

Accuracy

❏ I got them all right!
❏ I missed a couple.
❏ I will practice these:
(List up to 5 facts.)

Efficiency

I used these strategies:

❏ Build on known facts
of x2, x5, x10
❏ Double x3, x4, x6
❏ Other

Time

I finished in:

_____

My next goal is:

_____

Name _____

My Score _____

Test Your Skills

7 x 8	9 x 9	10 x 8	6 x 9	8 x 7	9 x 8
9 x 6	8 x 9	12 x 5	9 x 7	11 x 7	8 x 8
10 x 7	11 x 5	8 x 7	10 x 6	12 x 6	7 x 9
11 x 6	12 x 5	9 x 8	10 x 8	8 x 9	6 x 9
7 x 8	10 x 7	7 x 9	11 x 5	9 x 9	11 x 7
8 x 8	11 x 6	9 x 6	10 x 6	12 x 6	9 x 7

How am I doing?

Accuracy

❑ I got them all right!
❑ I missed a couple.
❑ I will practice these:
(List up to 5 facts.)

Efficiency

I used these strategies:
❑ Build on known facts
  of x2, x5, x10
❑ Double x3, x4, x6
❑ Other

Time

I finished in:

_____

My next goal is:

_____

Building Math Fluency • EMC 3035 • © Evan-Moor Corp.

Name _____   My Score _____

Test Your Skills

11 x 6	9 x 9	11 x 7	9 x 6	10 x 6	8 x 8
8 x 7	12 x 6	10 x 8	7 x 8	12 x 5	7 x 9
10 x 7	9 x 8	11 x 5	9 x 7	8 x 9	11 x 6
7 x 9	10 x 6	12 x 5	9 x 9	6 x 9	7 x 8
8 x 8	8 x 9	11 x 7	7 x 8	12 x 6	11 x 5
9 x 6	12 x 6	10 x 7	9 x 8	10 x 8	8 x 7

How am I doing?

Accuracy
❏ I got them all right!
❏ I missed a couple.
❏ I will practice these:
(List up to 5 facts.)

Efficiency
I used these strategies:
❏ Build on known facts
  of x2, x5, x10
❏ Double x3, x4, x6
❏ Other

Time
I finished in:
_____
My next goal is:
_____

Name _____   My Score _____

Test Your Skills

11 x 8	12 x 7	11 x 9	10 x 9	12 x 11	12 x 9
12 x 12	12 x 8	10 x 10	12 x 10	12 x 8	11 x 10
10 x 11	12 x 7	11 x 9	12 x 12	11 x 8	12 x 9
12 x 10	11 x 10	12 x 8	10 x 12	11 x 12	12 x 10
12 x 9	12 x 12	10 x 10	12 x 11	12 x 7	10 x 11
11 x 11	12 x 11	12 x 8	10 x 12	12 x 12	12 x 9

How am I doing?

Accuracy
❏ I got them all right!
❏ I missed a couple.
❏ I will practice these:
(List up to 5 facts.)

Efficiency
I used these strategies:
❏ Build on known facts
   of x2, x5, x10
❏ Double x3, x4, x6
❏ Other

Time
I finished in:

_____

My next goal is:

_____

   Building Math Fluency • EMC 3035 • © Evan-Moor Corp.

Name _____   My Score _____

Test Your Skills

2 × 2	3 × 4	5 × 6	2 × 9	6 × 7	4 × 5
3 × 9	5 × 8	3 × 6	8 × 8	2 × 5	6 × 9
7 × 7	4 × 6	2 × 3	4 × 9	3 × 8	8 × 9
2 × 4	3 × 7	4 × 4	3 × 3	5 × 9	7 × 8
5 × 5	4 × 8	2 × 6	6 × 8	2 × 8	9 × 9
2 × 7	6 × 6	5 × 7	3 × 5	4 × 7	7 × 9

How am I doing?

Accuracy

❏ I got them all right!
❏ I missed a couple.
❏ I will practice these:
(List up to 5 facts.)

Efficiency

I used these strategies:

❏ Build on known facts
 of x2, x5, x10
❏ Double x3, x4, x6
❏ Other

Time

I finished in:

_____

My next goal is:

_____

Name _____   My Score _____

Test Your Skills

9	12	8	6	10	6
x 3	x 5	x 8	x 3	x 9	x 5

11	4	3	7	9	10
x 8	x 3	x 8	x 6	x 4	x 10

9	12	12	10	12	7
x 6	x 12	x 11	x 12	x 6	x 3

5	12	9	8	11	9
x 4	x 7	x 7	x 7	x 9	x 5

9	8	12	11	9	7
x 8	x 6	x 8	x 12	x 9	x 4

7	10	6	8	12	5
x 7	x 11	x 4	x 4	x 9	x 3

How am I doing?

Accuracy
❏ I got them all right!
❏ I missed a couple.
❏ I will practice these:
(List up to 5 facts.)

Efficiency
I used these strategies:
❏ Build on known facts
   of x2, x5, x10
❏ Double x3, x4, x6
❏ Other

Time
I finished in:
_____

My next goal is:
_____

Name _____ My Score _____

Test Your Skills

$4 \div 2 =$ _____ $0 \div 7 =$ _____ $0 \div 12 =$ _____

$0 \div 10 =$ _____ $3 \div 3 =$ _____ $8 \div 4 =$ _____

$3 \div 1 =$ _____ $10 \div 1 =$ _____ $9 \div 9 =$ _____

$1 \div 1 =$ _____ $10 \div 2 =$ _____ $9 \div 3 =$ _____

$8 \div 2 =$ _____ $0 \div 3 =$ _____ $6 \div 6 =$ _____

$9 \div 1 =$ _____ $2 \div 1 =$ _____ $4 \div 2 =$ _____

$8 \div 1 =$ _____ $6 \div 2 =$ _____ $4 \div 4 =$ _____

$0 \div 9 =$ _____ $0 \div 11 =$ _____ $7 \div 1 =$ _____

$4 \div 1 =$ _____ $10 \div 10 =$ _____ $8 \div 8 =$ _____

$9 \div 9 =$ _____ $8 \div 4 =$ _____ $5 \div 5 =$ _____

$6 \div 1 =$ _____ $2 \div 2 =$ _____ $7 \div 7 =$ _____

$10 \div 5 =$ _____ $6 \div 3 =$ _____ $8 \div 2 =$ _____

How am I doing?

Accuracy

❏ I got them all right!
❏ I missed a couple.
❏ I will practice these:
(List up to 5 facts.)

Efficiency

I used these strategies:
❏ Division of 0
❏ Divide by 1
❏ Divide by Self
❏ Doubles Facts

Time

I finished in:

_____

My next goal is:

_____

Name _____   My Score _____

Test Your Skills

$12 \div 12 =$ _____ $18 \div 9 =$ _____ $20 \div 2 =$ _____

$21 \div 7 =$ _____ $24 \div 4 =$ _____ $25 \div 5 =$ _____

$24 \div 3 =$ _____ $18 \div 2 =$ _____ $12 \div 1 =$ _____

$24 \div 12 =$ _____ $12 \div 4 =$ _____ $18 \div 6 =$ _____

$20 \div 5 =$ _____ $24 \div 8 =$ _____ $12 \div 6 =$ _____

$12 \div 2 =$ _____ $24 \div 6 =$ _____ $20 \div 4 =$ _____

$18 \div 3 =$ _____ $11 \div 1 =$ _____ $24 \div 2 =$ _____

$14 \div 2 =$ _____ $15 \div 5 =$ _____ $16 \div 4 =$ _____

$16 \div 2 =$ _____ $22 \div 2 =$ _____ $12 \div 3 =$ _____

$20 \div 10 =$ _____ $11 \div 11 =$ _____ $24 \div 3 =$ _____

$22 \div 11 =$ _____ $16 \div 8 =$ _____ $12 \div 1 =$ _____

$15 \div 3 =$ _____ $14 \div 7 =$ _____ $21 \div 3 =$ _____

How am I doing?

Accuracy
❏ I got them all right!
❏ I missed a couple.
❏ I will practice these:
(List up to 5 facts.)

Efficiency
I used these strategies:
❏ Divide by 1
❏ Divide by Self
❏ Doubles Facts
❏ Think Multiplication

Time
I finished in:
_____
My next goal is:
_____

Name _____   My Score _____

Test Your Skills

$12 \div 2 =$ _____ $24 \div 3 =$ _____ $24 \div 12 =$ _____

$15 \div 3 =$ _____ $22 \div 11 =$ _____ $20 \div 10 =$ _____

$24 \div 6 =$ _____ $24 \div 8 =$ _____ $12 \div 4 =$ _____

$14 \div 7 =$ _____ $16 \div 8 =$ _____ $11 \div 11 =$ _____

$21 \div 3 =$ _____ $12 \div 1 =$ _____ $18 \div 2 =$ _____

$24 \div 2 =$ _____ $16 \div 4 =$ _____ $18 \div 6 =$ _____

$20 \div 2 =$ _____ $25 \div 5 =$ _____ $12 \div 1 =$ _____

$12 \div 3 =$ _____ $12 \div 6 =$ _____ $20 \div 4 =$ _____

$11 \div 1 =$ _____ $15 \div 5 =$ _____ $22 \div 2 =$ _____

$18 \div 9 =$ _____ $24 \div 4 =$ _____ $20 \div 5 =$ _____

$18 \div 3 =$ _____ $14 \div 2 =$ _____ $16 \div 2 =$ _____

$12 \div 12 =$ _____ $21 \div 7 =$ _____ $24 \div 3 =$ _____

How am I doing?

Accuracy
❏ I got them all right!
❏ I missed a couple.
❏ I will practice these:
(List up to 5 facts.)

Efficiency
I used these strategies:
❏ Divide by 1
❏ Divide by Self
❏ Doubles Facts
❏ Think Multiplication

Time
I finished in:

_____

My next goal is:

_____

Name _____ My Score _____

Test Your Skills

$28 \div 4 =$ _____ $50 \div 10 =$ _____ $36 \div 6 =$ _____

$30 \div 6 =$ _____ $48 \div 8 =$ _____ $40 \div 4 =$ _____

$45 \div 5 =$ _____ $30 \div 5 =$ _____ $42 \div 7 =$ _____

$42 \div 6 =$ _____ $32 \div 4 =$ _____ $36 \div 3 =$ _____

$30 \div 3 =$ _____ $48 \div 4 =$ _____ $27 \div 3 =$ _____

$32 \div 8 =$ _____ $33 \div 3 =$ _____ $44 \div 11 =$ _____

$40 \div 10 =$ _____ $33 \div 11 =$ _____ $36 \div 4 =$ _____

$36 \div 12 =$ _____ $35 \div 7 =$ _____ $40 \div 5 =$ _____

$40 \div 8 =$ _____ $49 \div 7 =$ _____ $28 \div 7 =$ _____

$27 \div 9 =$ _____ $36 \div 9 =$ _____ $44 \div 4 =$ _____

$35 \div 5 =$ _____ $30 \div 10 =$ _____ $48 \div 12 =$ _____

$45 \div 9 =$ _____ $48 \div 6 =$ _____ $50 \div 5 =$ _____

How am I doing?

Accuracy
❑ I got them all right!
❑ I missed a couple.
❑ I will practice these:
(List up to 5 facts.)

Efficiency
I used these strategies:
❑ Think Multiplication
❑ Other

Time
I finished in:
_____
My next goal is:
_____

Test Your Skills

$45 \div 5 =$ _____ $28 \div 7 =$ _____ $27 \div 9 =$ _____

$36 \div 6 =$ _____ $40 \div 5 =$ _____ $44 \div 4 =$ _____

$33 \div 11 =$ _____ $30 \div 6 =$ _____ $48 \div 8 =$ _____

$50 \div 5 =$ _____ $32 \div 8 =$ _____ $33 \div 3 =$ _____

$28 \div 4 =$ _____ $42 \div 6 =$ _____ $40 \div 10 =$ _____

$30 \div 5 =$ _____ $40 \div 4 =$ _____ $32 \div 4 =$ _____

$36 \div 3 =$ _____ $44 \div 11 =$ _____ $30 \div 10 =$ _____

$48 \div 6 =$ _____ $36 \div 12 =$ _____ $35 \div 7 =$ _____

$35 \div 5 =$ _____ $36 \div 4 =$ _____ $48 \div 12 =$ _____

$27 \div 3 =$ _____ $49 \div 7 =$ _____ $30 \div 3 =$ _____

$40 \div 8 =$ _____ $36 \div 9 =$ _____ $50 \div 10 =$ _____

$45 \div 9 =$ _____ $42 \div 7 =$ _____ $48 \div 4 =$ _____

How am I doing?

Accuracy
- ❏ I got them all right!
- ❏ I missed a couple.
- ❏ I will practice these:
(List up to 5 facts.)

Efficiency
I used these strategies:
- ❏ Think Multiplication
- ❏ Other

Time
I finished in:

_____

My next goal is:

_____

Name _____   My Score _____

Test Your Skills

$56 \div 7 =$ _____ $80 \div 10 =$ _____ $60 \div 5 =$ _____

$72 \div 12 =$ _____ $63 \div 9 =$ _____ $77 \div 11 =$ _____

$70 \div 7 =$ _____ $56 \div 8 =$ _____ $64 \div 8 =$ _____

$66 \div 11 =$ _____ $54 \div 9 =$ _____ $72 \div 8 =$ _____

$77 \div 7 =$ _____ $63 \div 7 =$ _____ $56 \div 7 =$ _____

$60 \div 10 =$ _____ $66 \div 6 =$ _____ $60 \div 12 =$ _____

$54 \div 6 =$ _____ $72 \div 9 =$ _____ $63 \div 9 =$ _____

$60 \div 5 =$ _____ $55 \div 11 =$ _____ $81 \div 9 =$ _____

$80 \div 8 =$ _____ $60 \div 6 =$ _____ $72 \div 6 =$ _____

$55 \div 5 =$ _____ $70 \div 10 =$ _____ $63 \div 7 =$ _____

$72 \div 8 =$ _____ $64 \div 8 =$ _____ $56 \div 8 =$ _____

$81 \div 9 =$ _____ $54 \div 6 =$ _____ $72 \div 9 =$ _____

How am I doing?

Accuracy
❏ I got them all right!
❏ I missed a couple.
❏ I will practice these:
(List up to 5 facts.)

Efficiency
I used these strategies:
❏ Think Multiplication
❏ Other

Time
I finished in:

_____

My next goal is:

_____

Name _____   My Score _____

Test Your Skills

56 ÷ 7 = _____   63 ÷ 7 = _____   81 ÷ 9 = _____

64 ÷ 8 = _____   72 ÷ 8 = _____   77 ÷ 7 = _____

80 ÷ 10 = _____   56 ÷ 8 = _____   55 ÷ 11 = _____

54 ÷ 6 = _____   70 ÷ 10 = _____   63 ÷ 7 = _____

81 ÷ 9 = _____   55 ÷ 5 = _____   60 ÷ 5 = _____

66 ÷ 11 = _____   60 ÷ 10 = _____   72 ÷ 9 = _____

54 ÷ 9 = _____   60 ÷ 5 = _____   72 ÷ 6 = _____

77 ÷ 11 = _____   72 ÷ 12 = _____   56 ÷ 8 = _____

63 ÷ 9 = _____   54 ÷ 9 = _____   64 ÷ 8 = _____

72 ÷ 6 = _____   60 ÷ 6 = _____   54 ÷ 6 = _____

60 ÷ 12 = _____   80 ÷ 8 = _____   63 ÷ 9 = _____

72 ÷ 12 = _____   56 ÷ 7 = _____   72 ÷ 9 = _____

How am I doing?

Accuracy
❏ I got them all right!
❏ I missed a couple.
❏ I will practice these:
(List up to 5 facts.)

Efficiency
I used these strategies:
❏ Think Multiplication
❏ Other

Time
I finished in:
_____
My next goal is:
_____

Name _____   My Score _____

Test Your Skills

$110 \div 10 =$ _____ $108 \div 9 =$ _____ $99 \div 9 =$ _____

$84 \div 12 =$ _____ $84 \div 7 =$ _____ $96 \div 12 =$ _____

$108 \div 9 =$ _____ $99 \div 11 =$ _____ $121 \div 11 =$ _____

$90 \div 9 =$ _____ $96 \div 8 =$ _____ $84 \div 7 =$ _____

$132 \div 12 =$ _____ $88 \div 8 =$ _____ $110 \div 10 =$ _____

$108 \div 12 =$ _____ $96 \div 12 =$ _____ $88 \div 11 =$ _____

$144 \div 12 =$ _____ $120 \div 10 =$ _____ $84 \div 12 =$ _____

$84 \div 7 =$ _____ $132 \div 11 =$ _____ $144 \div 12 =$ _____

$90 \div 10 =$ _____ $84 \div 12 =$ _____ $132 \div 11 =$ _____

$120 \div 12 =$ _____ $108 \div 12 =$ _____ $110 \div 11 =$ _____

$99 \div 9 =$ _____ $100 \div 10 =$ _____ $88 \div 11 =$ _____

$110 \div 11 =$ _____ $84 \div 7 =$ _____ $120 \div 10 =$ _____

How am I doing?

Accuracy
❏ I got them all right!
❏ I missed a couple.
❏ I will practice these:
(List up to 5 facts.)

Efficiency
I used these strategies:
❏ Think Multiplication
❏ Other

Time
I finished in:

_____

My next goal is:

_____

Name _____   My Score _____

Test Your Skills

$4 \div 2 =$ _____ $49 \div 7 =$ _____ $25 \div 5 =$ _____

$12 \div 3 =$ _____ $24 \div 4 =$ _____ $32 \div 4 =$ _____

$30 \div 5 =$ _____ $6 \div 2 =$ _____ $12 \div 2 =$ _____

$18 \div 2 =$ _____ $36 \div 4 =$ _____ $48 \div 6 =$ _____

$42 \div 6 =$ _____ $24 \div 3 =$ _____ $16 \div 2 =$ _____

$20 \div 4 =$ _____ $72 \div 8 =$ _____ $81 \div 9 =$ _____

$27 \div 3 =$ _____ $8 \div 2 =$ _____ $14 \div 2 =$ _____

$40 \div 5 =$ _____ $21 \div 3 =$ _____ $36 \div 6 =$ _____

$18 \div 3 =$ _____ $16 \div 4 =$ _____ $35 \div 5 =$ _____

$64 \div 8 =$ _____ $9 \div 3 =$ _____ $28 \div 4 =$ _____

$24 \div 6 =$ _____ $45 \div 5 =$ _____ $63 \div 7 =$ _____

$54 \div 6 =$ _____ $56 \div 7 =$ _____ $15 \div 3 =$ _____

How am I doing?

Accuracy
❑ I got them all right!
❑ I missed a couple.
❑ I will practice these:
(List up to 5 facts.)

Efficiency
I used these strategies:
❑ Think Multiplication
❑ Other

Time
I finished in:

_____

My next goal is:

_____

Name _____ My Score _____

Test Your Skills

$27 \div 9 =$ _____ $54 \div 9 =$ _____ $72 \div 9 =$ _____

$60 \div 12 =$ _____ $144 \div 12 =$ _____ $40 \div 8 =$ _____

$64 \div 8 =$ _____ $132 \div 12 =$ _____ $96 \div 12 =$ _____

$18 \div 6 =$ _____ $108 \div 9 =$ _____ $132 \div 11 =$ _____

$90 \div 10 =$ _____ $72 \div 12 =$ _____ $81 \div 9 =$ _____

$30 \div 6 =$ _____ $21 \div 7 =$ _____ $28 \div 7 =$ _____

$88 \div 11 =$ _____ $20 \div 5 =$ _____ $49 \div 7 =$ _____

$12 \div 4 =$ _____ $84 \div 12 =$ _____ $110 \div 10 =$ _____

$24 \div 8 =$ _____ $63 \div 9 =$ _____ $24 \div 6 =$ _____

$42 \div 7 =$ _____ $48 \div 8 =$ _____ $32 \div 8 =$ _____

$36 \div 9 =$ _____ $99 \div 11 =$ _____ $108 \div 12 =$ _____

$100 \div 10 =$ _____ $15 \div 5 =$ _____ $36 \div 9 =$ _____

How am I doing?

Accuracy
❏ I got them all right!
❏ I missed a couple.
❏ I will practice these:
(List up to 5 facts.)

Efficiency
I used these strategies:
❏ Think Multiplication
❏ Other

Time
I finished in:

_____

My next goal is:

_____

Facts Flashcards

Practice with flashcards can help students gain automaticity with math facts. Flashcards enable students to work at their own pace and to focus on the specific facts that they need to learn.

Prepare the Flashcards

- Reproduce the cards that students need to practice. Within each operation, the cards progress from easier to more difficult facts. Keep the cards to a manageable number; add new cards as facts are mastered.

- Students cut the cards apart and write the answers on the backs of the cards. Be sure to check the answers so that students do not practice the wrong answers.

- Store the cards in an envelope or self-sealing plastic bag.

- Use the template on page 146 if you wish to create flashcards for a specific strategy or for individual needs.

Tips for Practicing the Flashcards

- When students practice independently, encourage them to softly say the facts aloud so they both see and hear them.

- Have students practice with a partner. This is more fun and it ensures that students are computing each answer and not just looking at the answer. If an answer is incorrect, the partner should say, for example, "No, $8 + 6$ is 14." Then the answering student should repeat the equation aloud.

- Have students sort and then practice the cards by the strategies they would use to compute the answers. Cards can be categorized into piles of:

Addition & Subtraction	**Multiplication & Division**
Easy Facts—Plus 1, Minus 0, Count Up	Easy Facts—Times 1, Divide by 0 or 1
Doubles	Doubles
Tens Partners	Triples
Plus or Minus 9 or 10	Think Times Ten
Hidden Doubles	Square Numbers
Fact Families	Fact Families

- Allow students to personalize their cards to show the strategies used to compute the answers.

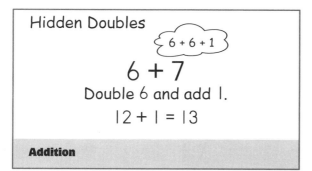

8 + 2	9 + 1	10 + 0	5 + 5
Addition	Addition	Addition	Addition
7 + 4	8 + 3	6 + 4	7 + 3
Addition	Addition	Addition	Addition
7 + 5	6 + 5	8 + 4	9 + 3
Addition	Addition	Addition	Addition
8 + 8	7 + 7	7 + 6	6 + 6
Addition	Addition	Addition	Addition

Building Math Fluency • EMC 3035 • © Evan-Moor Corp.

9 + 6	12 + 4	8 + 6	11 + 3
Addition	Addition	Addition	Addition
9 + 7	9 + 5	8 + 7	8 + 5
Addition	Addition	Addition	Addition
9 + 9	15 + 5	9 + 8	11 + 5
Addition	Addition	Addition	Addition
9 + 4	13 + 7	10 + 9	12 + 6
Addition	Addition	Addition	Addition

$12 - 6$	$10 - 9$	$11 - 8$	$10 - 5$
Subtraction	Subtraction	Subtraction	Subtraction
$12 - 8$	$10 - 6$	$11 - 7$	$10 - 7$
Subtraction	Subtraction	Subtraction	Subtraction
$13 - 5$	$11 - 6$	$12 - 7$	$10 - 4$
Subtraction	Subtraction	Subtraction	Subtraction
$16 - 8$	$14 - 7$	$13 - 6$	$11 - 5$
Subtraction	Subtraction	Subtraction	Subtraction

$16 - 7$	$14 - 6$
Subtraction	Subtraction
$17 - 9$	$14 - 9$
Subtraction	Subtraction
$13 - 7$	$15 - 7$
Subtraction	Subtraction
$13 - 9$	$15 - 9$
Subtraction	Subtraction

$16 - 9$	$14 - 8$
Subtraction	Subtraction
$17 - 8$	$14 - 5$
Subtraction	Subtraction
$18 - 9$	$15 - 6$
Subtraction	Subtraction
$13 - 8$	$15 - 8$
Subtraction	Subtraction

3×2		
2×3		4×4
Multiplication		5×4
		4×5

3×2
2×3

Multiplication

4×4

Multiplication

5×4
4×5

Multiplication

6×6

Multiplication

2×2

Multiplication

4×3
3×4

Multiplication

5×3
3×5

Multiplication

6×3
3×6

Multiplication

0×7
7×0

Multiplication

4×2
2×4

Multiplication

5×2
2×5

Multiplication

6×2
2×6

Multiplication

1×9
9×1

3×3

Multiplication

5×1
1×5

Multiplication

5×5

Multiplication

Multiplication

6×4 4×6

6×5 5×6

7×2 2×7

Multiplication

7×3 3×7

7×4 4×7

7×7

Multiplication

7×5 5×7

7×6 6×7

Multiplication

8×2 2×8

8×3 3×8

8×4 4×8

Multiplication

8×5 5×8

Multiplication

8×6 6×8

8×7 7×8

8×8

Multiplication

9×2 2×9

9 × 6
6 × 9

Multiplication

1 × 10
10 × 1

Multiplication

5 × 10
10 × 5

Multiplication

10 × 9
9 × 10

Multiplication

9 × 5
5 × 9

Multiplication

9 × 9

Multiplication

4 × 10
10 × 4

Multiplication

8 × 10
10 × 8

Multiplication

9 × 4
4 × 9

Multiplication

9 × 8
8 × 9

Multiplication

3 × 10
10 × 3

Multiplication

7 × 10
10 × 7

Multiplication

9 × 3
3 × 9

Multiplication

9 × 7
7 × 9

Multiplication

2 × 10
10 × 2

Multiplication

6 × 10
10 × 6

Multiplication

Building Math Fluency • EMC 3035 • © Evan-Moor Corp.

$0 \div 3$	$4 \div 2$	$7 \div 7$
Division	Division	Division
$6 \div 3$	$6 \div 2$	$5 \div 5$
Division	Division	Division
$10 \div 2$	$9 \div 3$	$8 \div 2$
Division	Division	Division
$12 \div 4$	$12 \div 3$	$12 \div 2$
Division	Division	Division

$0 \div 9$
Division
$5 \div 1$
Division
$8 \div 4$
Division
$10 \div 5$
Division

$15 \div 3$	$14 \div 7$	$14 \div 2$
Division	Division	Division
$18 \div 9$	$16 \div 2$	$16 \div 8$
Division	Division	Division
$20 \div 4$	$18 \div 6$	$18 \div 3$
Division	Division	Division
$21 \div 7$	$20 \div 10$	$20 \div 2$
Division	Division	Division

$12 \div 6$

Division

$15 \div 5$

Division

$18 \div 2$

Division

$20 \div 5$

Division

$21 \div 3$	$24 \div 6$	$24 \div 4$	$24 \div 8$
Division	Division	Division	Division
$24 \div 3$	$25 \div 5$	$27 \div 3$	$27 \div 9$
Division	Division	Division	Division
$28 \div 4$	$28 \div 7$	$30 \div 10$	$30 \div 3$
Division	Division	Division	Division
$30 \div 5$	$30 \div 6$	$32 \div 8$	$32 \div 4$
Division	Division	Division	Division

$36 \div 9$	$40 \div 8$	$45 \div 9$	$50 \div 5$
Division	Division	Division	Division
$36 \div 4$	$40 \div 5$	$45 \div 5$	$49 \div 7$
Division	Division	Division	Division
$35 \div 5$	$40 \div 4$	$42 \div 7$	$48 \div 6$
Division	Division	Division	Division
$35 \div 7$	$40 \div 10$	$42 \div 6$	$48 \div 8$
Division	Division	Division	Division

$63 \div 7$	$54 \div 9$	$54 \div 6$	$50 \div 10$
Division	Division	Division	Division
$70 \div 10$	$70 \div 7$	$64 \div 8$	$63 \div 9$
Division	Division	Division	Division
$80 \div 8$	$81 \div 9$	$72 \div 9$	$72 \div 8$
Division	Division	Division	Division
$100 \div 10$	$90 \div 10$	$81 \div 9$	$80 \div 10$
Division	Division	Division	Division

Strategy:

Strategy:

Strategy:

Strategy:

Strategy:

Strategy:

Strategy:

Strategy:

Strategy:

Strategy:

Strategy:

Strategy:

Answer Key

Page 8

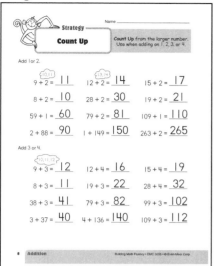

Count Up — Count Up from the larger number. Use when adding on 1, 2, 3, or 4.

Add 1 or 2.

$9 + 2 = 11$ $12 + 2 = 14$ $15 + 2 = 17$

$8 + 2 = 10$ $28 + 2 = 30$ $19 + 2 = 21$

$59 + 1 = 60$ $79 + 2 = 81$ $109 + 1 = 110$

$2 + 88 = 90$ $1 + 149 = 150$ $263 + 2 = 265$

Add 3 or 4.

$9 + 3 = 12$ $12 + 4 = 16$ $15 + 4 = 19$

$8 + 3 = 11$ $19 + 3 = 22$ $28 + 4 = 32$

$38 + 3 = 41$ $79 + 3 = 82$ $99 + 3 = 102$

$3 + 37 = 40$ $4 + 136 = 140$ $109 + 3 = 112$

Page 9

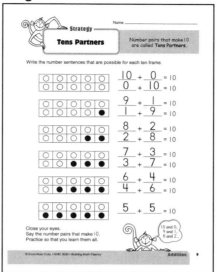

Tens Partners — Number pairs that make 10 are called **Tens Partners**.

Write the number sentences that are possible for each ten frame.

$10 + 0 = 10$
$0 + 10 = 10$

$9 + 1 = 10$
$1 + 9 = 10$

$8 + 2 = 10$
$2 + 8 = 10$

$7 + 3 = 10$
$3 + 7 = 10$

$6 + 4 = 10$
$4 + 6 = 10$

$5 + 5 = 10$

Close your eyes.
Say the number pairs that make 10.
Practice so that you learn them all.

10 and 0.
9 and 1.
8 and 2...

Page 10

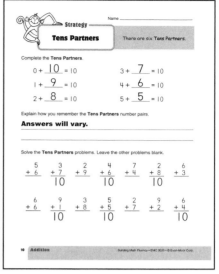

Tens Partners — There are six Tens Partners.

Complete the **Tens Partners**.

$0 + 10 = 10$ $3 + 7 = 10$

$1 + 9 = 10$ $4 + 6 = 10$

$2 + 8 = 10$ $5 + 5 = 10$

Explain how you remember the **Tens Partners** number pairs.

Answers will vary.

Solve the **Tens Partners** problems. Leave the other problems blank.

$\begin{array}{c}5\\+6\\\hline\end{array}$ $\begin{array}{c}3\\+7\\\hline 10\end{array}$ $\begin{array}{c}2\\+9\\\hline\end{array}$ $\begin{array}{c}4\\+6\\\hline 10\end{array}$ $\begin{array}{c}7\\+4\\\hline\end{array}$ $\begin{array}{c}2\\+8\\\hline 10\end{array}$ $\begin{array}{c}6\\+3\\\hline\end{array}$

$\begin{array}{c}6\\+6\\\hline\end{array}$ $\begin{array}{c}9\\+1\\\hline 10\end{array}$ $\begin{array}{c}3\\+8\\\hline\end{array}$ $\begin{array}{c}5\\+5\\\hline 10\end{array}$ $\begin{array}{c}2\\+7\\\hline\end{array}$ $\begin{array}{c}9\\+2\\\hline\end{array}$ $\begin{array}{c}6\\+4\\\hline 10\end{array}$

Page 11

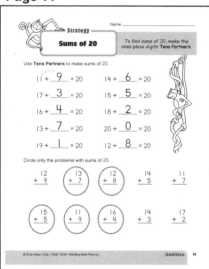

Sums of 20 — To find sums of 20, make the ones-place digits **Tens Partners**.

Use Tens Partners to make sums of 20.

$11 + 9 = 20$ $14 + 6 = 20$

$17 + 3 = 20$ $15 + 5 = 20$

$16 + 4 = 20$ $18 + 2 = 20$

$13 + 7 = 20$ $20 + 0 = 20$

$19 + 1 = 20$ $12 + 8 = 20$

Circle only the problems with sums of 20.

$\begin{array}{c}12\\+9\\\hline\end{array}$ $\boxed{\begin{array}{c}13\\+7\\\hline\end{array}}$ $\boxed{\begin{array}{c}12\\+8\\\hline\end{array}}$ $\begin{array}{c}14\\+5\\\hline\end{array}$ $\begin{array}{c}11\\+7\\\hline\end{array}$

$\boxed{\begin{array}{c}15\\+5\\\hline\end{array}}$ $\boxed{\begin{array}{c}11\\+9\\\hline\end{array}}$ $\boxed{\begin{array}{c}16\\+4\\\hline\end{array}}$ $\begin{array}{c}14\\+3\\\hline\end{array}$ $\begin{array}{c}17\\+2\\\hline\end{array}$

Page 12

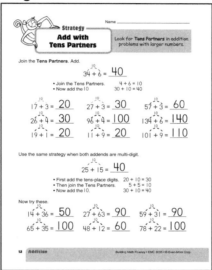

Add with Tens Partners — Look for **Tens Partners** in addition problems with larger numbers.

Join the **Tens Partners**. Add.

$34 + 6 = 40$

• Join the Tens Partners. $4 + 6 = 10$
• Now add the 10 $30 + 10 = 40$

$17 + 3 = 20$ $27 + 3 = 30$ $57 + 3 = 60$

$26 + 4 = 30$ $96 + 4 = 100$ $134 + 6 = 140$

$19 + 1 = 20$ $11 + 9 = 20$ $101 + 9 = 110$

Use the same strategy when both addends are multi-digit.

$25 + 15 = 40$

• First add the tens-place digits. $20 + 10 = 30$
• Then join the Tens Partners. $5 + 5 = 10$
• Now add the 10. $30 + 10 = 40$

Now try these.

$14 + 36 = 50$ $27 + 63 = 90$ $59 + 31 = 90$

$65 + 35 = 100$ $48 + 12 = 60$ $78 + 22 = 100$

Page 13

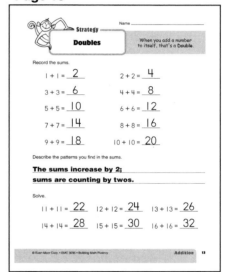

Doubles — When you add a number to itself, that's a **Double**.

Record the sums.

$1 + 1 = 2$ $2 + 2 = 4$

$3 + 3 = 6$ $4 + 4 = 8$

$5 + 5 = 10$ $6 + 6 = 12$

$7 + 7 = 14$ $8 + 8 = 16$

$9 + 9 = 18$ $10 + 10 = 20$

Describe the patterns you find in the sums.

The sums increase by 2;
sums are counting by twos.

Solve.

$11 + 11 = 22$ $12 + 12 = 24$ $13 + 13 = 26$

$14 + 14 = 28$ $15 + 15 = 30$ $16 + 16 = 32$

Page 14

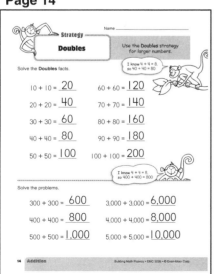

Doubles — Use the Doubles strategy for larger numbers.

Solve the **Doubles** facts.

I know $4 + 4 = 8$, so $40 + 40 = 80$.

$10 + 10 = 20$ $60 + 60 = 120$

$20 + 20 = 40$ $70 + 70 = 140$

$30 + 30 = 60$ $80 + 80 = 160$

$40 + 40 = 80$ $90 + 90 = 180$

$50 + 50 = 100$ $100 + 100 = 200$

I know $4 + 4 = 8$, so $400 + 400 = 800$.

Solve the problems.

$300 + 300 = 600$ $3,000 + 3,000 = 6,000$

$400 + 400 = 800$ $4,000 + 4,000 = 8,000$

$500 + 500 = 1,000$ $5,000 + 5,000 = 10,000$

Page 15

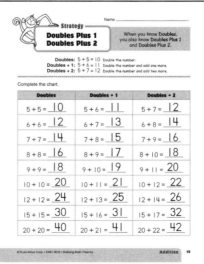

Doubles Plus 1 / Doubles Plus 2 — When you know Doubles, you also know Doubles Plus 1 and Doubles Plus 2.

Doubles: $5 + 5 = 10$ double the number.
Doubles + 1: $5 + 6 = 11$ double the number and add one more.
Doubles + 2: $5 + 7 = 12$ double the number and add two more.

Complete the chart.

Doubles	Doubles + 1	Doubles + 2
$5 + 5 = 10$	$5 + 6 = 11$	$5 + 7 = 12$
$6 + 6 = 12$	$6 + 7 = 13$	$6 + 8 = 14$
$7 + 7 = 14$	$7 + 8 = 15$	$7 + 9 = 16$
$8 + 8 = 16$	$8 + 9 = 17$	$8 + 10 = 18$
$9 + 9 = 18$	$9 + 10 = 19$	$9 + 11 = 20$
$10 + 10 = 20$	$10 + 11 = 21$	$10 + 12 = 22$
$12 + 12 = 24$	$12 + 13 = 25$	$12 + 14 = 26$
$15 + 15 = 30$	$15 + 16 = 31$	$15 + 17 = 32$
$20 + 20 = 40$	$20 + 21 = 41$	$20 + 22 = 42$

Page 16

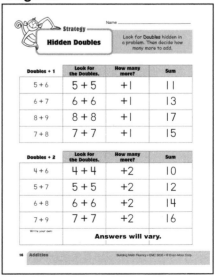

Hidden Doubles — Look for Doubles hidden in a problem. Then decide how many more to add.

Doubles + 1	Look for the Doubles.	How many more?	Sum
$5 + 6$	$5 + 5$	$+1$	11
$6 + 7$	$6 + 6$	$+1$	13
$8 + 9$	$8 + 8$	$+1$	17
$7 + 8$	$7 + 7$	$+1$	15

Doubles + 2	Look for the Doubles.	How many more?	Sum
$4 + 6$	$4 + 4$	$+2$	10
$5 + 7$	$5 + 5$	$+2$	12
$6 + 8$	$6 + 6$	$+2$	14
$7 + 9$	$7 + 7$	$+2$	16
Write your own	**Answers will vary.**		

Page 17

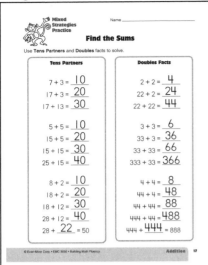

Mixed Strategies Practice

Find the Sums

Name _____

Use **Tens Partners** and **Doubles** facts to solve.

Tens Partners	Doubles Facts
$7 + 3 = 10$	$2 + 2 = 4$
$17 + 3 = 20$	$22 + 2 = 24$
$17 + 13 = 30$	$22 + 22 = 44$
$5 + 5 = 10$	$3 + 3 = 6$
$15 + 5 = 20$	$33 + 3 = 36$
$15 + 15 = 30$	$33 + 33 = 66$
$25 + 15 = 40$	$333 + 33 = 366$
$8 + 2 = 10$	$4 + 4 = 8$
$18 + 2 = 20$	$44 + 4 = 48$
$18 + 12 = 30$	$44 + 44 = 88$
$28 + 12 = 40$	$444 + 44 = 488$
$28 + 22 = 50$	$444 + 444 = 888$

© Evan-Moor Corp. • EMC 3035 • Building Math Fluency   Addition 17

Page 18

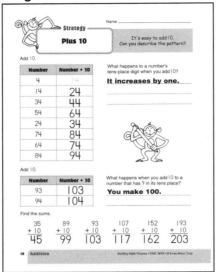

Strategy

Plus 10

It's easy to add 10. Can you describe the pattern?

Add 10.

Number	Number + 10
4	14
14	24
34	44
54	64
24	34
74	84
64	74
84	94

What happens to a number's tens-place digit when you add 10?

It increases by one.

Add 10.

Number	Number + 10
93	103
94	104

What happens when you add 10 to a number that has 9 in its tens place?

You make 100.

Find the sums.

35 $+ 10$	89 $+ 10$	93 $+ 10$	107 $+ 10$	152 $+ 10$	193 $+ 10$
45	99	103	117	162	203

18 Addition   Building Math Fluency • EMC 3035 • © Evan-Moor Corp.

Page 19

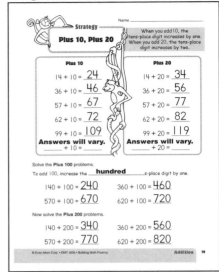

Strategy

Plus 10, Plus 20

When you add 10, the tens-place digit increases by one. When you add 20, the tens-place digit increases by two.

Plus 10	Plus 20
$14 + 10 = 24$	$14 + 20 = 34$
$36 + 10 = 46$	$36 + 20 = 56$
$57 + 10 = 67$	$57 + 20 = 77$
$62 + 10 = 72$	$62 + 20 = 82$
$99 + 10 = 109$	$99 + 20 = 119$
Answers will vary.	**Answers will vary.**
$+ 10 =$	$+ 20 =$

Solve the **Plus 100** problems.
To add 100, increase the **hundred** s-place digit by one.

$140 + 100 = 240$	$360 + 100 = 460$
$570 + 100 = 670$	$620 + 100 = 720$

Now solve the **Plus 200** problems.

$140 + 200 = 340$	$360 + 200 = 560$
$570 + 200 = 770$	$620 + 200 = 820$

© Evan-Moor Corp. • EMC 3035 • Building Math Fluency   Addition 19

Page 20

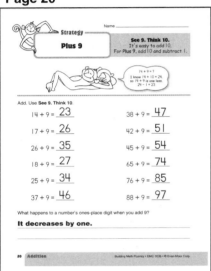

Strategy

Plus 9

See 9. Think 10.
It's easy to add 10. For Plus 9, add 10 and subtract 1.

$14 + 9 = ?$
I know $14 + 10 = 24$, so $14 + 9$ is one less. $24 - 1 = 23$

Add. Use **See 9. Think 10.**

$14 + 9 = 23$	$38 + 9 = 47$
$17 + 9 = 26$	$42 + 9 = 51$
$26 + 9 = 35$	$45 + 9 = 54$
$18 + 9 = 27$	$65 + 9 = 74$
$25 + 9 = 34$	$76 + 9 = 85$
$37 + 9 = 46$	$88 + 9 = 97$

What happens to a number's ones-place digit when you add 9?

It decreases by one.

20 Addition   Building Math Fluency • EMC 3035 • © Evan-Moor Corp.

Page 21

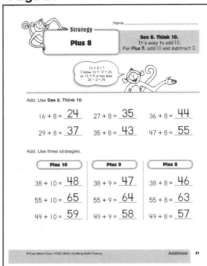

Strategy

Plus 8

See 8. Think 10.
It's easy to add 10. For Plus 8, add 10 and subtract 2.

$16 + 8 = ?$
I know $16 + 10 = 26$, so $16 + 8$ is two less. $26 - 2 = 24$

Add. Use **See 8. Think 10.**

$16 + 8 = 24$	$27 + 8 = 35$	$36 + 8 = 44$
$29 + 8 = 37$	$35 + 8 = 43$	$47 + 8 = 55$

Add. Use three strategies.

Plus 10	Plus 9	Plus 8
$38 + 10 = 48$	$38 + 9 = 47$	$38 + 8 = 46$
$55 + 10 = 65$	$55 + 9 = 64$	$55 + 8 = 63$
$49 + 10 = 59$	$49 + 9 = 58$	$49 + 8 = 57$

© Evan-Moor Corp. • EMC 3035 • Building Math Fluency   Addition 21

Page 22

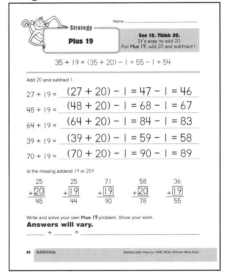

Strategy

Plus 19

See 19. Think 20.
It's easy to add 20. For Plus 19, add 20 and subtract 1.

$35 + 19 = (35 + 20) - 1 = 55 - 1 = 54$

Add 20 and subtract 1.

$27 + 19 = (27 + 20) - 1 = 47 - 1 = 46$
$48 + 19 = (48 + 20) - 1 = 68 - 1 = 67$
$64 + 19 = (64 + 20) - 1 = 84 - 1 = 83$
$39 + 19 = (39 + 20) - 1 = 59 - 1 = 58$
$70 + 19 = (70 + 20) - 1 = 90 - 1 = 89$

Is the missing addend 19 or 20?

25 $+ \boxed{20}$	25 $+ \boxed{19}$	71 $+ \boxed{19}$	58 $+ \boxed{20}$	36 $+ \boxed{19}$
45	44	90	78	55

Write and solve your own **Plus 19** problem. Show your work.

Answers will vary.

_____ + _____ = _____

22 Addition   Building Math Fluency • EMC 3035 • © Evan-Moor Corp.

Page 23

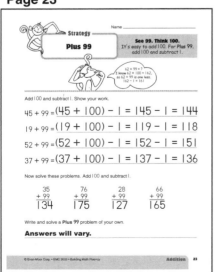

Strategy

Plus 99

See 99. Think 100.
It's easy to add 100. For Plus 99, add 100 and subtract 1.

$62 + 99 = ?$
I know $62 + 100 = 162$, so $62 + 99$ is one less. $162 - 1 = 161$

Add 100 and subtract 1. Show your work.

$45 + 99 = (45 + 100) - 1 = 145 - 1 = 144$
$19 + 99 = (19 + 100) - 1 = 119 - 1 = 118$
$52 + 99 = (52 + 100) - 1 = 152 - 1 = 151$
$37 + 99 = (37 + 100) - 1 = 137 - 1 = 136$

Now solve these problems. Add 100 and subtract 1.

35 $+ 99$	76 $+ 99$	28 $+ 99$	66 $+ 99$
134	175	127	165

Write and solve a **Plus 99** problem of your own.

Answers will vary.

© Evan-Moor Corp. • EMC 3035 • Building Math Fluency   Addition 23

Page 24

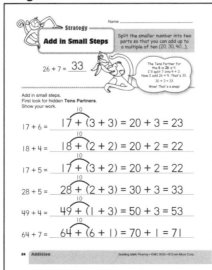

Strategy

Add in Small Steps

Split the smaller number into two parts so that you can add up to a multiple of ten (20, 30, 40...).

$26 + 7 = 33$

The Tens Partner for the 6 in 26 is 4. I'll split 7 into 4 + 3. Now I add $26 + 4$. That's 30. $30 + 3 = 33$. Wow! That's a snap!

Add in small steps.
First look for hidden **Tens Partners**. Show your work.

$17 + 6 = 17 + (3 + 3) = 20 + 3 = 23$
$18 + 4 = 18 + (2 + 2) = 20 + 2 = 22$
$17 + 5 = 17 + (3 + 2) = 20 + 2 = 22$
$28 + 5 = 28 + (2 + 3) = 30 + 3 = 33$
$49 + 4 = 49 + (1 + 3) = 50 + 3 = 53$
$64 + 7 = 64 + (6 + 1) = 70 + 1 = 71$

24 Addition   Building Math Fluency • EMC 3035 • © Evan-Moor Corp.

Page 25

Mixed Strategies Practice

Which Strategy Fits?

Strategy Names

Doubles   Doubles + 1   Doubles + 2   Tens-Partners   Plus 10   Plus 9

Solve the problems.
Write the strategy name.

Strategy name **Tens Partners**	Strategy name **Plus 10**	Strategy name **Plus 9**
$1 + 9 = 10$	$7 + 10 = 17$	$7 + 9 = 16$
$4 + 6 = 10$	$4 + 10 = 14$	$4 + 9 = 13$
$7 + 3 = 10$	$5 + 10 = 15$	$5 + 9 = 14$
$2 + 8 = 10$	$17 + 10 = 27$	$17 + 9 = 26$
$10 + 0 = 10$	$26 + 10 = 36$	$26 + 9 = 35$
	$48 + 10 = 58$	$48 + 9 = 57$

Strategy name **Doubles**	Strategy name **Doubles + 1**	Strategy name **Doubles + 2**
$6 + 6 = 12$	$6 + 7 = 13$	$7 + 9 = 16$
$7 + 7 = 14$	$7 + 8 = 15$	$8 + 10 = 18$
$8 + 8 = 16$	$8 + 9 = 17$	$6 + 8 = 14$
$9 + 9 = 18$	$9 + 10 = 19$	$5 + 7 = 12$
$12 + 12 = 24$	$12 + 13 = 25$	$12 + 14 = 26$
$25 + 25 = 50$	$25 + 26 = 51$	$25 + 27 = 52$

© Evan-Moor Corp. • EMC 3035 • Building Math Fluency   Addition 25

Page 26

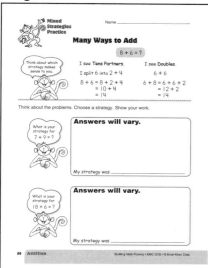

Mixed Strategies Practice

Many Ways to Add

$8 + 6 = ?$

Think about which strategy makes sense to you.

I see **Tens Partners**.
I split 6 into 2 + 4
$8 + 6 = 8 + 2 + 4$
$= 10 + 4$
$= 14$

I see **Doubles**.
$6 + 6$
$6 + 8 = 6 + 6 + 2$
$= 12 + 2$
$= 14$

Think about the problems. Choose a strategy. Show your work.

What is your strategy for $7 + 9 = ?$
Answers will vary.
My strategy was

What is your strategy for $18 + 6 = ?$
Answers will vary.
My strategy was

26 Addition

Page 27

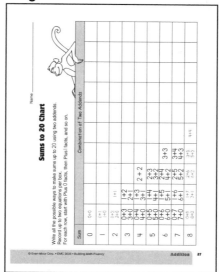

Sums to 20 Chart

Combination of Two Addends

Write all the possible ways to make sums up to 20 using two addends.
Record up to two equations per box.
For each row, start with Plus 0 facts, then Plus 1 facts, and so on.

Page 28

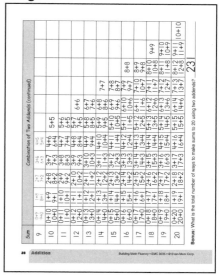

Combination of Two Addends (continued)

Bonus: What is the total number of ways to make sums to 20 using two addends? **23**

28 Addition

Page 31

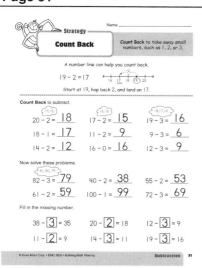

Strategy — Count Back

Count Back to take away small numbers, such as 1, 2, or 3.

A number line can help you count back.
$19 - 2 = 17$
Start at 19, hop back 2, and land on 17.

Count Back to subtract.
$20 - 2 = 18$ $17 - 2 = 15$ $19 - 3 = 16$
$18 - 1 = 17$ $11 - 2 = 9$ $9 - 3 = 6$
$14 - 2 = 12$ $16 - 0 = 16$ $12 - 3 = 9$

Now solve these problems.
$82 - 3 = 79$ $40 - 2 = 38$ $55 - 2 = 53$
$61 - 2 = 59$ $100 - 1 = 99$ $72 - 3 = 69$

Fill in the missing number.
$38 - \boxed{3} = 35$ $20 - \boxed{2} = 18$ $12 - \boxed{3} = 9$
$11 - \boxed{2} = 9$ $14 - \boxed{3} = 11$ $19 - \boxed{3} = 16$

Subtraction 31

Page 32

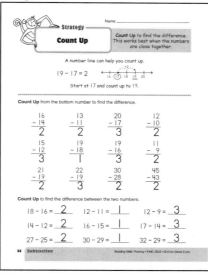

Strategy — Count Up

Count Up to find the difference. This works best when the numbers are close together.

A number line can help you count up.
$19 - 17 = 2$
Start at 17 and count up to 19.

Count Up from the bottom number to find the difference.
$16 - 14 = 2$ $13 - 11 = 2$ $20 - 17 = 3$ $12 - 10 = 2$
$15 - 12 = 3$ $19 - 18 = 1$ $19 - 16 = 3$ $11 - 9 = 2$
$21 - 19 = 2$ $22 - 19 = 3$ $30 - 28 = 2$ $45 - 43 = 2$

Count Up to find the difference between the two numbers.
$18 - 16 = 2$ $12 - 11 = 1$ $12 - 9 = 3$
$14 - 12 = 2$ $16 - 15 = 1$ $17 - 14 = 3$
$27 - 25 = 2$ $30 - 29 = 1$ $32 - 29 = 3$

32 Subtraction

Page 33

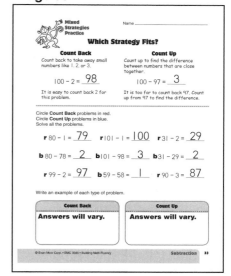

Mixed Strategies Practice

Which Strategy Fits?

Count Back
Count back to take away small numbers like 1, 2, or 3.
$100 - 2 = 98$
It is easy to count back 2 for this problem.

Count Up
Count up to find the difference between numbers that are close together.
$100 - 97 = 3$
It is too far to count back 97. Count up from 97 to find the difference.

Circle **Count Back** problems in red.
Circle **Count Up** problems in blue.
Solve all the problems.

r $80 - 1 = 79$ **r** $101 - 1 = 100$ **r** $31 - 2 = 29$
b $80 - 78 = 2$ **b** $101 - 98 = 3$ **b** $31 - 29 = 2$
r $99 - 2 = 97$ **b** $59 - 58 = 1$ **r** $90 - 3 = 87$

Write an example of each type of problem.

Count Back	Count Up
Answers will vary.	Answers will vary.

Subtraction 33

Page 34

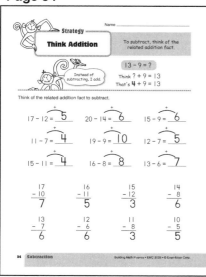

Strategy — Think Addition

To subtract, think of the related addition fact.

$13 - 9 = ?$
Instead of subtracting, I add.
Think $? + 9 = 13$
That's $4 + 9 = 13$

Think of the related addition fact to subtract.
$17 - 12 = 5$ $20 - 14 = 6$ $15 - 9 = 6$
$11 - 7 = 4$ $19 - 9 = 10$ $12 - 7 = 5$
$15 - 11 = 4$ $16 - 8 = 8$ $13 - 6 = 7$

$17 - 7 = 10$ $16 - 11 = 5$ $15 - 12 = 3$ $14 - 8 = 6$
$13 - 7 = 6$ $12 - 6 = 6$ $11 - 8 = 3$ $10 - 5 = 5$

34 Subtraction

Page 35

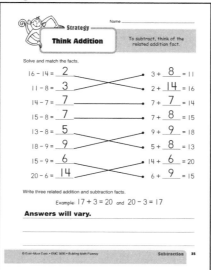

Strategy — Think Addition

To subtract, think of the related addition fact.

Solve and match the facts.
$16 - 14 = 2$ $3 + 8 = 11$
$11 - 8 = 3$ $2 + 14 = 16$
$14 - 7 = 7$ $7 + 7 = 14$
$15 - 8 = 7$ $7 + 8 = 15$
$13 - 8 = 5$ $9 + 9 = 18$
$18 - 9 = 9$ $5 + 8 = 13$
$15 - 9 = 6$ $14 + 6 = 20$
$20 - 6 = 14$ $6 + 9 = 15$

Write three related addition and subtraction facts.
Example: $17 + 3 = 20$ and $20 - 3 = 17$
Answers will vary.

Subtraction 35

Page 36

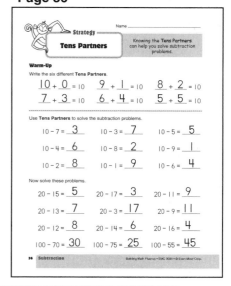

Strategy — Tens Partners

Knowing the **Tens Partners** can help you solve subtraction problems.

Warm-Up
Write the six different **Tens Partners**.
$10 + 0 = 10$ $9 + 1 = 10$ $8 + 2 = 10$
$7 + 3 = 10$ $6 + 4 = 10$ $5 + 5 = 10$

Use **Tens Partners** to solve the subtraction problems.
$10 - 7 = 3$ $10 - 3 = 7$ $10 - 5 = 5$
$10 - 4 = 6$ $10 - 8 = 2$ $10 - 9 = 1$
$10 - 2 = 8$ $10 - 1 = 9$ $10 - 6 = 4$

Now solve these problems.
$20 - 15 = 5$ $20 - 17 = 3$ $20 - 11 = 9$
$20 - 13 = 7$ $20 - 3 = 17$ $20 - 9 = 11$
$20 - 12 = 8$ $20 - 14 = 6$ $20 - 16 = 4$
$100 - 70 = 30$ $100 - 75 = 25$ $100 - 55 = 45$

36 Subtraction

Page 37

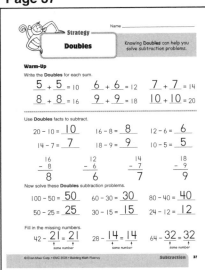

Strategy: Doubles

Knowing Doubles can help you solve subtraction problems.

Warm-Up

Write the Doubles for each sum.

$5 + 5 = 10$ $6 + 6 = 12$ $7 + 7 = 14$
$8 + 8 = 16$ $9 + 9 = 18$ $10 + 10 = 20$

Use Doubles facts to subtract.

$20 - 10 = 10$ $16 - 8 = 8$ $12 - 6 = 6$
$14 - 7 = 7$ $18 - 9 = 9$ $10 - 5 = 5$

$16 - 8 = 8$ $12 - 6 = 6$ $14 - 7 = 7$ $18 - 9 = 9$

Now solve these Doubles subtraction problems.

$100 - 50 = 50$ $60 - 30 = 30$ $80 - 40 = 40$
$50 - 25 = 25$ $30 - 15 = 15$ $24 - 12 = 12$

Fill in the missing numbers.

$42 - 21 = 21$ $28 - 14 = 14$ $64 - 32 = 32$
(same number) (same number) (same number)

Page 38

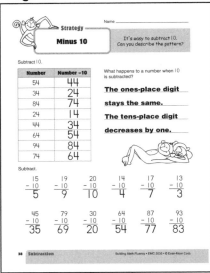

Strategy: Minus 10

It's easy to subtract 10. Can you describe the pattern?

Subtract 10.

Number	Number −10
54	44
34	24
84	74
24	14
44	34
64	54
94	84
74	64

What happens to a number when 10 is subtracted?

The ones-place digit stays the same.

The tens-place digit decreases by one.

Subtract.

$15 - 10 = 5$ $19 - 10 = 9$ $20 - 10 = 10$ $14 - 10 = 4$ $17 - 10 = 7$ $13 - 10 = 3$

$45 - 10 = 35$ $79 - 10 = 69$ $30 - 10 = 20$ $64 - 10 = 54$ $87 - 10 = 77$ $93 - 10 = 83$

Page 39

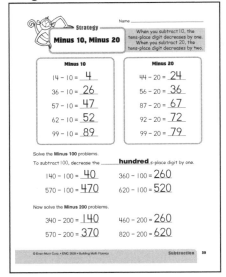

Strategy: Minus 10, Minus 20

When you subtract 10, the tens-place digit decreases by one. When you subtract 20, the tens-place digit decreases by two.

Minus 10	Minus 20
$14 - 10 = 4$	$44 - 20 = 24$
$36 - 10 = 26$	$56 - 20 = 36$
$57 - 10 = 47$	$87 - 20 = 67$
$62 - 10 = 52$	$92 - 20 = 72$
$99 - 10 = 89$	$99 - 20 = 79$

Solve the Minus 100 problems.
To subtract 100, decrease the **hundred**s-place digit by one.

$140 - 100 = 40$ $360 - 100 = 260$
$570 - 100 = 470$ $620 - 100 = 520$

Now solve the Minus 200 problems.

$340 - 200 = 140$ $460 - 200 = 260$
$570 - 200 = 370$ $820 - 200 = 620$

Page 40

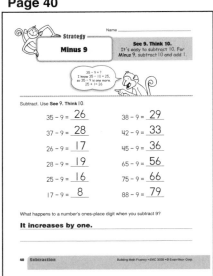

Strategy: Minus 9

See 9. Think 10. It's easy to subtract 10. For Minus 9, subtract 10 and add 1.

$35 - 9 = ?$
I know $35 - 10 = 25$, so $35 - 9$ is one more. $25 + 1 = 26$

Subtract. Use See 9. Think 10.

$35 - 9 = 26$ $38 - 9 = 29$
$37 - 9 = 28$ $42 - 9 = 33$
$26 - 9 = 17$ $45 - 9 = 36$
$28 - 9 = 19$ $65 - 9 = 56$
$25 - 9 = 16$ $75 - 9 = 66$
$17 - 9 = 8$ $88 - 9 = 79$

What happens to a number's ones-place digit when you subtract 9?

It increases by one.

Page 41

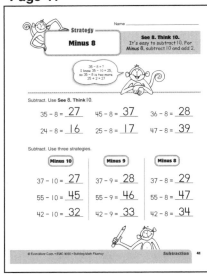

Strategy: Minus 8

See 8. Think 10. It's easy to subtract 10. For Minus 8, subtract 10 and add 2.

$35 - 8 = ?$
I know $35 - 10 = 25$, so $35 - 8$ is two more. $25 + 2 = 27$

Subtract. Use See 8. Think 10.

$35 - 8 = 27$ $45 - 8 = 37$ $36 - 8 = 28$
$24 - 8 = 16$ $25 - 8 = 17$ $47 - 8 = 39$

Subtract. Use three strategies.

Minus 10	Minus 9	Minus 8
$37 - 10 = 27$	$37 - 9 = 28$	$37 - 8 = 29$
$55 - 10 = 45$	$55 - 9 = 46$	$55 - 8 = 47$
$42 - 10 = 32$	$42 - 9 = 33$	$42 - 8 = 34$

Page 42

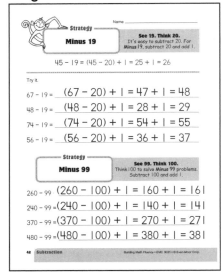

Strategy: Minus 19

See 19. Think 20. It's easy to subtract 20. For Minus 19, subtract 20 and add 1.

$45 - 19 = (45 - 20) + 1 = 25 + 1 = 26$

Try it.

$67 - 19 = (67 - 20) + 1 = 47 + 1 = 48$
$48 - 19 = (48 - 20) + 1 = 28 + 1 = 29$
$74 - 19 = (74 - 20) + 1 = 54 + 1 = 55$
$56 - 19 = (56 - 20) + 1 = 36 + 1 = 37$

Strategy: Minus 99

See 99. Think 100. Think 100 to solve Minus 99 problems. Subtract 100 and add 1.

$260 - 99 = (260 - 100) + 1 = 160 + 1 = 161$
$240 - 99 = (240 - 100) + 1 = 140 + 1 = 141$
$370 - 99 = (370 - 100) + 1 = 270 + 1 = 271$
$480 - 99 = (480 - 100) + 1 = 380 + 1 = 381$

Page 43

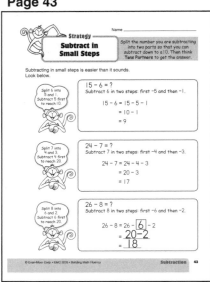

Strategy: Subtract in Small Steps

Split the number you are subtracting into two parts so that you can subtract down to a 10. Then think Tens Partners to get the answer.

Subtracting in small steps is easier than it sounds. Look below.

Split 6 into 5 and 1. Subtract 5 first to reach 10.

$15 - 6 = ?$
Subtract 6 in two steps: first −5 and then −1.
$15 - 6 = 15 - 5 - 1$
$= 10 - 1$
$= 9$

Split 7 into 4 and 3. Subtract 4 first to reach 20.

$24 - 7 = ?$
Subtract 7 in two steps: first −4 and then −3.
$24 - 7 = 24 - 4 - 3$
$= 20 - 3$
$= 17$

Split 8 into 6 and 2. Subtract 6 first to reach 20.

$26 - 8 = ?$
Subtract 8 in two steps: first −6 and then −2.
$26 - 8 = 26 - \boxed{6} - 2$
$= 20 - 2$
$= 18$

Page 44

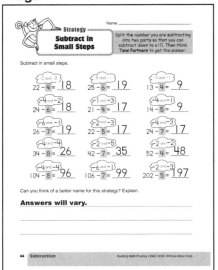

Strategy: Subtract in Small Steps

Split the number you are subtracting into two parts so that you can subtract down to a 10. Then think Tens Partners to get the answer.

Subtract in small steps.

$22 - 4 = 18$ (−2 and −2) $25 - 6 = 19$ (−5 and −1) $13 - 4 = 9$ (−3 and −1)
$24 - 6 = 18$ (−4 and −2) $21 - 4 = 17$ (−1 and −3) $14 - 5 = 9$ (−4 and −1)
$26 - 7 = 19$ (−6 and −1) $22 - 5 = 17$ (−2 and −3) $24 - 7 = 17$ (−4 and −3)
$34 - 8 = 26$ (−4 and −4) $43 - 8 = 35$ (−3 and −5) $52 - 4 = 48$ (−2 and −2)
$104 - 8 = 96$ (−4 and −4) $106 - 7 = 99$ (−6 and −1) $202 - 5 = 197$ (−2 and −3)

Can you think of a better name for this strategy? Explain.

Answers will vary.

Page 45

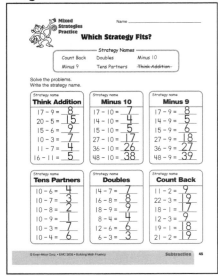

Mixed Strategies Practice: Which Strategy Fits?

Strategy Names: Count Back, Doubles, Minus 10, Minus 9, Tens Partners, ~~Think Addition~~

Solve the problems. Write the strategy name.

Strategy name **Think Addition**	Strategy name **Minus 10**	Strategy name **Minus 9**
$17 - 9 = 8$	$17 - 10 = 7$	$17 - 9 = 8$
$20 - 5 = 15$	$14 - 10 = 4$	$14 - 9 = 5$
$15 - 6 = 9$	$15 - 10 = 5$	$15 - 9 = 6$
$10 - 3 = 7$	$17 - 10 = 7$	$27 - 9 = 18$
$11 - 7 = 4$	$36 - 10 = 26$	$36 - 9 = 27$
$16 - 11 = 5$	$48 - 10 = 38$	$48 - 9 = 39$

Strategy name **Tens Partners**	Strategy name **Doubles**	Strategy name **Count Back**
$10 - 6 = 4$	$14 - 7 = 7$	$11 - 2 = 9$
$10 - 7 = 3$	$16 - 8 = 8$	$22 - 3 = 19$
$10 - 8 = 2$	$18 - 9 = 9$	$12 - 3 = 9$
$10 - 9 = 1$	$8 - 4 = 4$	$19 - 1 = 18$
$10 - 3 = 7$	$12 - 6 = 6$	$21 - 2 = 19$
$10 - 4 = 6$	$6 - 3 = 3$	

Page 46

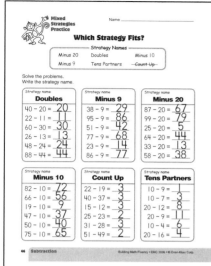

Name _____

Which Strategy Fits?

Strategy Names
Minus 20   Doubles   Minus 10
Minus 9   Tens Partners   Count Up

Solve the problems.
Write the strategy name.

Strategy name **Doubles**
40 − 20 = 20
22 − 11 = 11
60 − 30 = 30
26 − 13 = 13
48 − 24 = 24
88 − 44 = 44

Strategy name **Minus 9**
38 − 9 = 29
95 − 9 = 86
51 − 9 = 42
77 − 9 = 68
23 − 9 = 14
86 − 9 = 77

Strategy name **Minus 20**
87 − 20 = 67
99 − 20 = 79
25 − 20 = 5
64 − 20 = 44
33 − 20 = 13
58 − 20 = 38

Strategy name **Minus 10**
82 − 10 = 72
66 − 10 = 56
19 − 10 = 9
47 − 10 = 37
50 − 10 = 40
75 − 10 = 65

Strategy name **Count Up**
22 − 19 = 3
40 − 37 = 3
15 − 12 = 3
25 − 23 = 2
31 − 28 = 3
51 − 49 = 2

Strategy name **Tens Partners**
10 − 9 = 1
10 − 7 = 3
20 − 12 = 8
20 − 9 = 11
20 − 3 = 17
20 − 16 = 4

46 Subtraction

Page 47

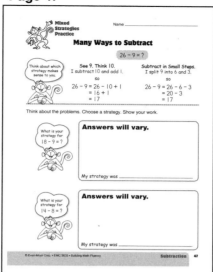

Name _____

Many Ways to Subtract

26 − 9 = ?

Think about which strategy makes sense to you.

See 9. Think 10.
I subtract 10 and add 1.
so
26 − 9 = 26 − 10 + 1
= 16 + 1
= 17

Subtract in Small Steps.
I split 9 into 6 and 3.
so
26 − 9 = 26 − 6 − 3
= 20 − 3
= 17

Think about the problems. Choose a strategy. Show your work.

What is your strategy for 18 − 9 = ?

Answers will vary.

My strategy was _____

What is your strategy for 14 − 8 = ?

Answers will vary.

My strategy was _____

Subtraction 47

Page 50

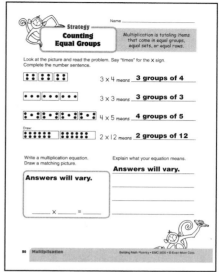

Strategy

Counting Equal Groups

Multiplication is totaling items that come in equal groups, equal sets, or equal rows.

Name _____

Look at the picture and read the problem. Say "times" for the x sign.
Complete the number sentence.

3 × 4 means **3 groups of 4**

3 × 3 means **3 groups of 3**

4 × 5 means **4 groups of 5**

Draw:
2 × 12 means **2 groups of 12**

Write a multiplication equation.
Draw a matching picture.

Answers will vary.

____ × ____ = ____

Explain what your equation means.

Answers will vary.

50 Multiplication

Page 51

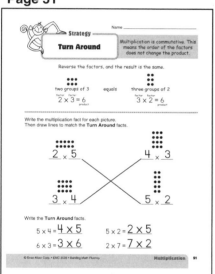

Strategy

Turn Around

Multiplication is commutative. This means the order of the factors does not change the product.

Name _____

Reverse the factors, and the result is the same.

two groups of 3   equals   three groups of 2
factor factor   factor factor
2 × 3 = 6 product   3 × 2 = 6 product

Write the multiplication fact for each picture.
Then draw lines to match the Turn Around facts.

2 × 5   4 × 3

3 × 4   5 × 2

Write the Turn Around facts.
5 × 4 = 4 × 5   5 × 2 = 2 × 5
6 × 3 = 3 × 6   2 × 7 = 7 × 2

Multiplication 51

Page 52

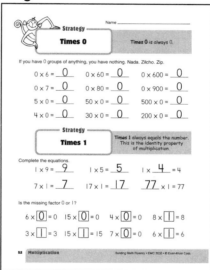

Strategy

Times 0

Times 0 is always 0.

Name _____

If you have 0 groups of anything, you have nothing. Nada. Zilcho. Zip.

0 × 6 = 0   0 × 60 = 0   0 × 600 = 0
0 × 7 = 0   0 × 80 = 0   0 × 900 = 0
5 × 0 = 0   50 × 0 = 0   500 × 0 = 0
4 × 0 = 0   30 × 0 = 0   200 × 0 = 0

Strategy

Times 1

Times 1 always equals the number. This is the identity property of multiplication.

Complete the equations.

1 × 9 = 9   1 × 5 = 5   1 × 4 = 4
7 × 1 = 7   17 × 1 = 17   77 × 1 = 77

Is the missing factor 0 or 1?

6 × 0 = 0   15 × 0 = 0   4 × 0 = 0   8 × 1 = 8
3 × 1 = 3   15 × 1 = 15   7 × 0 = 0   6 × 1 = 6

52 Multiplication

Page 53

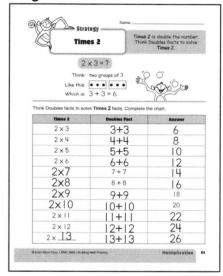

Strategy

Times 2

Times 2 is double the number. Think Doubles to solve Times 2.

Name _____

2 × 3 = ?

Think: two groups of 3
Like this: ● ● ● ● ● ●
Which is: 3 + 3 = 6

Think Doubles facts to solve Times 2 facts. Complete the chart.

Times 2	Doubles Fact	Answer
2 × 3	3+3	6
2 × 4	4+4	8
2 × 5	5+5	10
2 × 6	6+6	12
2 × 7	7 + 7	14
2 × 8	8 + 8	16
2 × 9	9+9	18
2 × 10	10+10	20
2 × 11	11+11	22
2 × 12	12+12	24
2 × 13	13+13	26

Multiplication 53

Page 54

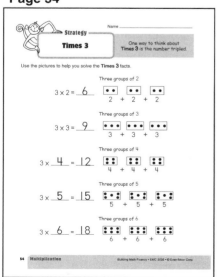

Strategy

Times 3

One way to think about Times 3 is the number tripled.

Name _____

Use the pictures to help you solve the Times 3 facts.

Three groups of 2
3 × 2 = 6   2 + 2 + 2

Three groups of 3
3 × 3 = 9   3 + 3 + 3

Three groups of 4
3 × 4 = 12   4 + 4 + 4

Three groups of 5
3 × 5 = 15   5 + 5 + 5

Three groups of 6
3 × 6 = 18   6 + 6 + 6

54 Multiplication

Page 55

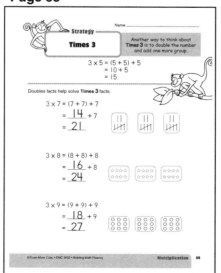

Strategy

Times 3

Another way to think about Times 3 is to double the number and add one more group.

Name _____

3 × 5 = (5 + 5) + 5
= 10 + 5
= 15

Doubles facts help solve Times 3 facts.

3 × 7 = (7 + 7) + 7
= 14 + 7
= 21

3 × 8 = (8 + 8) + 8
= 16 + 8
= 24

3 × 9 = (9 + 9) + 9
= 18 + 9
= 27

Multiplication 55

Page 56

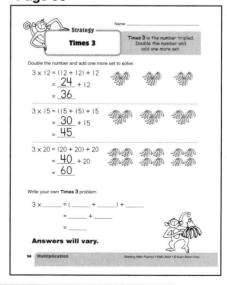

Strategy

Times 3

Times 3 is the number tripled. Double the number and add one more set.

Name _____

Double the number and add one more set to solve.

3 × 12 = (12 + 12) + 12
= 24 + 12
= 36

3 × 15 = (15 + 15) + 15
= 30 + 15
= 45

3 × 20 = (20 + 20) + 20
= 40 + 20
= 60

Write your own Times 3 problem.

3 × ____ = (____ + ____) + ____
= ____
= ____

Answers will vary.

56 Multiplication

Page 57

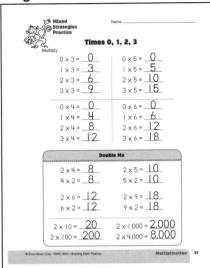

Mixed Strategies Practice

Times 0, 1, 2, 3

Multiply.

0 × 3 = 0   0 × 5 = 0
1 × 3 = 3   1 × 5 = 5
2 × 3 = 6   2 × 5 = 10
3 × 3 = 9   3 × 5 = 15

0 × 4 = 0   0 × 6 = 0
1 × 4 = 4   1 × 6 = 6
2 × 4 = 8   2 × 6 = 12
3 × 4 = 12   3 × 6 = 18

Double Me

2 × 4 = 8   4 × 2 = 10
4 × 2 = 8   5 × 2 = 10
2 × 6 = 12   2 × 9 = 18
6 × 2 = 12   9 × 2 = 18
2 × 10 = 20   2 × 1,000 = 2,000
2 × 100 = 200   2 × 4,000 = 8,000

Page 58

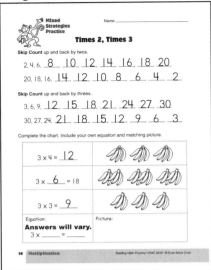

Mixed Strategies Practice

Times 2, Times 3

Skip Count up and back by twos.

2, 4, 6, 8, 10, 12, 14, 16, 18, 20
20, 18, 16, 14, 12, 10, 8, 6, 4, 2

Skip Count up and back by threes.

3, 6, 9, 12, 15, 18, 21, 24, 27, 30
30, 27, 24, 21, 18, 15, 12, 9, 6, 3

Complete the chart. Include your own equation and matching picture.

3 × 4 = 12
3 × 6 = 18
3 × 3 = 9

Equation: **Answers will vary.**
3 × ___ = ___

Picture:

Page 59

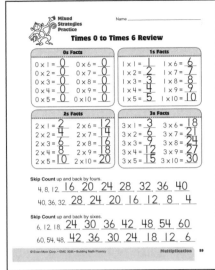

Mixed Strategies Practice

Times 0 to Times 6 Review

0s Facts		1s Facts	
0 × 1 = 0	0 × 6 = 0	1 × 1 = 1	1 × 6 = 6
0 × 2 = 0	0 × 7 = 0	1 × 2 = 2	1 × 7 = 7
0 × 3 = 0	0 × 8 = 0	1 × 3 = 3	1 × 8 = 8
0 × 4 = 0	0 × 9 = 0	1 × 4 = 4	1 × 9 = 9
0 × 5 = 0	0 × 10 = 0	1 × 5 = 5	1 × 10 = 10

2s Facts		3s Facts	
2 × 1 = 2	2 × 6 = 12	3 × 1 = 3	3 × 6 = 18
2 × 2 = 4	2 × 7 = 14	3 × 2 = 6	3 × 7 = 21
2 × 3 = 6	2 × 8 = 16	3 × 3 = 9	3 × 8 = 24
2 × 4 = 8	2 × 9 = 18	3 × 4 = 12	3 × 9 = 27
2 × 5 = 10	2 × 10 = 20	3 × 5 = 15	3 × 10 = 30

Skip Count up and back by fours.

4, 8, 12, 16, 20, 24, 28, 32, 36, 40
40, 36, 32, 28, 24, 20, 16, 12, 8, 4

Skip Count up and back by sixes.

6, 12, 18, 24, 30, 36, 42, 48, 54, 60
60, 54, 48, 42, 36, 30, 24, 18, 12, 6

Page 60

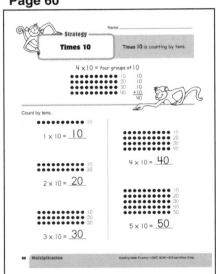

Strategy

Times 10   Times 10 is counting by tens.

4 × 10 = four groups of 10

Count by tens.

1 × 10 = 10
2 × 10 = 20
3 × 10 = 30
4 × 10 = 40
5 × 10 = 50

Page 61

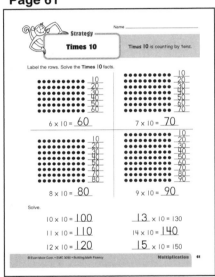

Strategy

Times 10   Times 10 is counting by tens.

Label the rows. Solve the Times 10 facts.

6 × 10 = 60   7 × 10 = 70
8 × 10 = 80   9 × 10 = 90

Solve.

10 × 10 = 100   13 × 10 = 130
11 × 10 = 110   14 × 10 = 140
12 × 10 = 120   15 × 10 = 150

Page 62

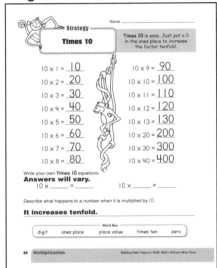

Strategy

Times 10   Times 10 is easy. Just put a 0 in the ones place to increase the factor tenfold.

10 × 1 = 10   10 × 9 = 90
10 × 2 = 20   10 × 10 = 100
10 × 3 = 30   10 × 11 = 110
10 × 4 = 40   10 × 12 = 120
10 × 5 = 50   10 × 13 = 130
10 × 6 = 60   10 × 20 = 200
10 × 7 = 70   10 × 30 = 300
10 × 8 = 80   10 × 40 = 400

Write your own Times 10 equations. **Answers will vary.**
10 × ___ = ___   10 × ___ = ___

Describe what happens to a number when it is multiplied by 10.

It increases tenfold.

Word Box
digit   ones place   place value   times ten   zero

Page 63

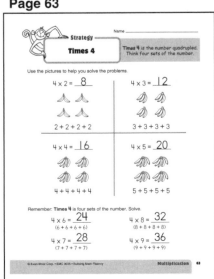

Strategy

Times 4   Times 4 is the number quadrupled. Think four sets of the number.

Use the pictures to help you solve the problems.

4 × 2 = 8   4 × 3 = 12
2 + 2 + 2 + 2   3 + 3 + 3 + 3

4 × 4 = 16   4 × 5 = 20
4 + 4 + 4 + 4   5 + 5 + 5 + 5

Remember: Times 4 is four sets of the number. Solve.

4 × 6 = 24   4 × 8 = 32
(6 + 6 + 6 + 6)   (8 + 8 + 8 + 8)
4 × 7 = 28   4 × 9 = 36
(7 + 7 + 7 + 7)   (9 + 9 + 9 + 9)

Page 64

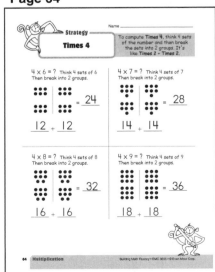

Strategy

Times 4   To compute Times 4, think 4 sets of the number and then break the sets into 2 groups. It's like Times 2 + Times 2.

4 × 6 = ? Think 4 sets of 6   4 × 7 = ? Think 4 sets of 7
Then break into 2 groups.   Then break into 2 groups.
= 24   = 28
12 + 12   14 + 14

4 × 8 = ? Think 4 sets of 8   4 × 9 = ? Think 4 sets of 9
Then break into 2 groups.   Then break into 2 groups.
= 32   = 36
16 + 16   18 + 18

Page 65

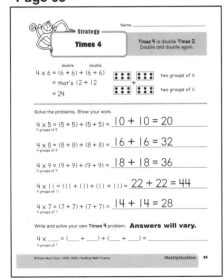

Strategy

Times 4   Times 4 is double Times 2. Double and double again.

         double   double
4 × 6 = (6 + 6) + (6 + 6)   two groups of 6
= that's 12 + 12   two groups of 6
= 24

Solve the problems. Show your work.

4 × 5 = (5 + 5) + (5 + 5) = 10 + 10 = 20
4 groups of 5

4 × 8 = (8 + 8) + (8 + 8) = 16 + 16 = 32
4 groups of 8

4 × 9 = (9 + 9) + (9 + 9) = 18 + 18 = 36
4 groups of 9

4 × 11 = (11 + 11) + (11 + 11) = 22 + 22 = 44
4 groups of 11

4 × 7 = (7 + 7) + (7 + 7) = 14 + 14 = 28
4 groups of 7

Write and solve your own Times 4 problem. **Answers will vary.**

4 × ___ = (___ + ___) + (___ + ___) = ___
4 groups of ___

Page 66

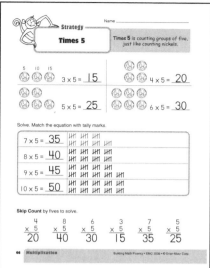

Strategy — Times 5 | Times 5 is counting groups of five, just like counting nickels.

5 10 15
$3 \times 5 = 15$ $4 \times 5 = 20$
$5 \times 5 = 25$ $6 \times 5 = 30$

Solve. Match the equation with tally marks.

$7 \times 5 = 35$
$8 \times 5 = 40$
$9 \times 5 = 45$
$10 \times 5 = 50$

Skip Count by fives to solve.

$\begin{array}{c}4\\ \times 5\\ \hline 20\end{array}$ $\begin{array}{c}8\\ \times 5\\ \hline 40\end{array}$ $\begin{array}{c}6\\ \times 5\\ \hline 30\end{array}$ $\begin{array}{c}3\\ \times 5\\ \hline 15\end{array}$ $\begin{array}{c}7\\ \times 5\\ \hline 35\end{array}$ $\begin{array}{c}5\\ \times 5\\ \hline 25\end{array}$

Page 67

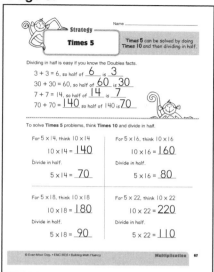

Strategy — Times 5 | Times 5 can be solved by doing Times 10 and then dividing in half.

Dividing in half is easy if you know the Doubles facts.
$3 + 3 = 6$, so half of 6 is 3
$30 + 30 = 60$, so half of 60 is 30
$7 + 7 = 14$, so half of 14 is 7
$70 + 70 = 140$, so half of 140 is 70

To solve **Times 5** problems, think **Times 10** and divide in half.

For 5×14, think 10×14
$10 \times 14 = 140$
Divide in half.
$5 \times 14 = 70$

For 5×16, think 10×16
$10 \times 16 = 160$
Divide in half.
$5 \times 16 = 80$

For 5×18, think 10×18
$10 \times 18 = 180$
Divide in half.
$5 \times 18 = 90$

For 5×22, think 10×22
$10 \times 22 = 220$
Divide in half.
$5 \times 22 = 110$

Page 68

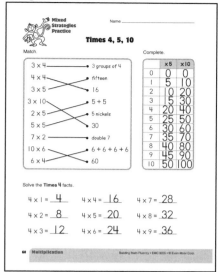

Mixed Strategies Practice — Times 4, 5, 10

Match.
3×4 — 3 groups of 4
4×4 — fifteen
3×5 — 16
3×10 — 5 + 5
2×5 — 5 nickels
5×5 — 30
7×2 — double 7
10×6 — 6 + 6 + 6 + 6
6×4 — 60

Complete.

	×5	×10
0	0	0
1	5	10
2	10	20
3	15	30
4	20	40
5	25	50
6	30	60
7	35	70
8	40	80
9	45	90
10	50	100

Solve the **Times 4** facts.

$4 \times 1 = 4$ $4 \times 4 = 16$ $4 \times 7 = 28$
$4 \times 2 = 8$ $4 \times 5 = 20$ $4 \times 8 = 32$
$4 \times 3 = 12$ $4 \times 6 = 24$ $4 \times 9 = 36$

Page 69

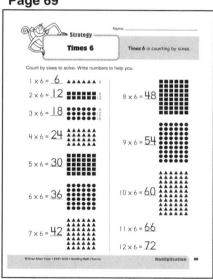

Strategy — Times 6 | Times 6 is counting by sixes.

Count by sixes to solve. Write numbers to help you.

$1 \times 6 = 6$
$2 \times 6 = 12$
$3 \times 6 = 18$
$4 \times 6 = 24$
$5 \times 6 = 30$
$6 \times 6 = 36$
$7 \times 6 = 42$
$8 \times 6 = 48$
$9 \times 6 = 54$
$10 \times 6 = 60$
$11 \times 6 = 66$
$12 \times 6 = 72$

Page 70

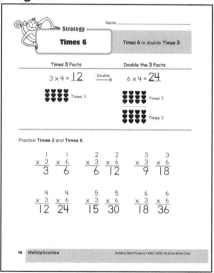

Strategy — Times 6 | Times 6 is double Times 3.

Times 3 Facts → Double the 3 Facts
$3 \times 4 = 12$ Double $6 \times 4 = 24$

Practice **Times 3** and **Times 6**.

$\begin{array}{c}1\\ \times 3\\ \hline 3\end{array}$ $\begin{array}{c}1\\ \times 6\\ \hline 6\end{array}$ $\begin{array}{c}2\\ \times 3\\ \hline 6\end{array}$ $\begin{array}{c}2\\ \times 6\\ \hline 12\end{array}$ $\begin{array}{c}3\\ \times 3\\ \hline 9\end{array}$ $\begin{array}{c}3\\ \times 6\\ \hline 18\end{array}$

$\begin{array}{c}4\\ \times 3\\ \hline 12\end{array}$ $\begin{array}{c}4\\ \times 6\\ \hline 24\end{array}$ $\begin{array}{c}5\\ \times 3\\ \hline 15\end{array}$ $\begin{array}{c}5\\ \times 6\\ \hline 30\end{array}$ $\begin{array}{c}6\\ \times 3\\ \hline 18\end{array}$ $\begin{array}{c}6\\ \times 6\\ \hline 36\end{array}$

Page 71

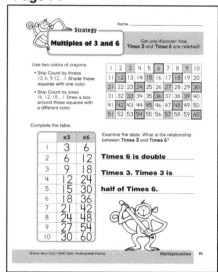

Strategy — Multiples of 3 and 6 | Can you discover how Times 3 and Times 6 are related?

Use two colors of crayons.
• Skip Count by threes (3, 6, 9, 12...) Shade these squares with one color.
• Skip Count by sixes (6, 12, 18...) Draw a box around these squares with a different color.

Complete the table.

	×3	×6
1	3	6
2	6	12
3	9	18
4	12	24
5	15	30
6	18	36
7	21	42
8	24	48
9	27	54
10	30	60

Examine the table. What is the relationship between **Times 3** and **Times 6**?

Times 6 is double Times 3. Times 3 is half of Times 6.

Page 72

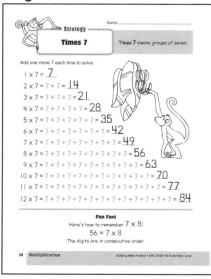

Strategy — Times 7 | Times 7 means groups of seven.

Add one more 7 each time to solve.

$1 \times 7 = 7$
$2 \times 7 = 7 + 7 = 14$
$3 \times 7 = 7 + 7 + 7 = 21$
$4 \times 7 = 7 + 7 + 7 + 7 = 28$
$5 \times 7 = 7 + 7 + 7 + 7 + 7 = 35$
$6 \times 7 = 7 + 7 + 7 + 7 + 7 + 7 = 42$
$7 \times 7 = 7 + 7 + 7 + 7 + 7 + 7 + 7 = 49$
$8 \times 7 = 7 + 7 + 7 + 7 + 7 + 7 + 7 + 7 = 56$
$9 \times 7 = 7 + 7 + 7 + 7 + 7 + 7 + 7 + 7 + 7 = 63$
$10 \times 7 = 7 + 7 + 7 + 7 + 7 + 7 + 7 + 7 + 7 + 7 = 70$
$11 \times 7 = 7 + 7 + 7 + 7 + 7 + 7 + 7 + 7 + 7 + 7 + 7 = 77$
$12 \times 7 = 7 + 7 + 7 + 7 + 7 + 7 + 7 + 7 + 7 + 7 + 7 + 7 = 84$

Fun Fact
Here's how to remember 7×8:
$56 = 7 \times 8$
The digits are in consecutive order.

Page 73

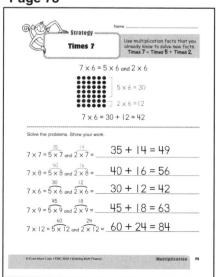

Strategy — Times 7 | Use multiplication facts that you already know to solve new facts. Times 7 = Times 5 + Times 2.

$7 \times 6 = 5 \times 6$ and 2×6
$5 \times 6 = 30$
$2 \times 6 = 12$
$7 \times 6 = 30 + 12 = 42$

Solve the problems. Show your work.

$7 \times 7 = 5 \times 7$ and $2 \times 7 = 35 + 14 = 49$
$7 \times 8 = 5 \times 8$ and $2 \times 8 = 40 + 16 = 56$
$7 \times 6 = 5 \times 6$ and $2 \times 6 = 30 + 12 = 42$
$7 \times 9 = 5 \times 9$ and $2 \times 9 = 45 + 18 = 63$
$7 \times 12 = 5 \times 12$ and $2 \times 12 = 60 + 24 = 84$

Page 74

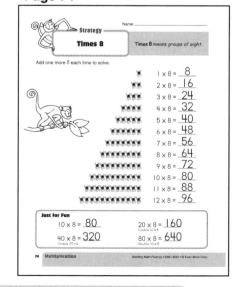

Strategy — Times 8 | Times 8 means groups of eight.

Add one more 8 each time to solve.

$1 \times 8 = 8$
$2 \times 8 = 16$
$3 \times 8 = 24$
$4 \times 8 = 32$
$5 \times 8 = 40$
$6 \times 8 = 48$
$7 \times 8 = 56$
$8 \times 8 = 64$
$9 \times 8 = 72$
$10 \times 8 = 80$
$11 \times 8 = 88$
$12 \times 8 = 96$

Just for Fun
$10 \times 8 = 80$ $20 \times 8 = 160$
$40 \times 8 = 320$ $80 \times 8 = 640$

Page 75

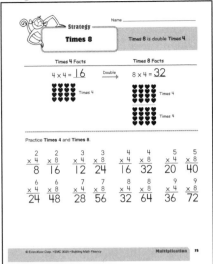

Strategy: **Times 8** — Times 8 is double Times 4.

Times 4 Facts	Times 8 Facts
$4 \times 4 = 16$	Double → $8 \times 4 = 32$

Times 4 / Times 8

Practice **Times 4** and **Times 8**.

$\begin{array}{c}2\\\times 4\\\hline 8\end{array}$ $\begin{array}{c}2\\\times 8\\\hline 16\end{array}$ $\begin{array}{c}3\\\times 4\\\hline 12\end{array}$ $\begin{array}{c}3\\\times 8\\\hline 24\end{array}$ $\begin{array}{c}4\\\times 4\\\hline 16\end{array}$ $\begin{array}{c}4\\\times 8\\\hline 32\end{array}$ $\begin{array}{c}5\\\times 4\\\hline 20\end{array}$ $\begin{array}{c}5\\\times 8\\\hline 40\end{array}$

$\begin{array}{c}6\\\times 4\\\hline 24\end{array}$ $\begin{array}{c}6\\\times 8\\\hline 48\end{array}$ $\begin{array}{c}7\\\times 4\\\hline 28\end{array}$ $\begin{array}{c}7\\\times 8\\\hline 56\end{array}$ $\begin{array}{c}8\\\times 4\\\hline 32\end{array}$ $\begin{array}{c}8\\\times 8\\\hline 64\end{array}$ $\begin{array}{c}9\\\times 4\\\hline 36\end{array}$ $\begin{array}{c}9\\\times 8\\\hline 72\end{array}$

Page 76

Strategy: **Multiples of 2, 4, and 8** — Can you discover how Times 2, Times 4, and Times 8 are related?

Use three colors of crayons.
- Skip Count by twos (2, 4, 6…) Shade these squares with one color.
- Skip Count by fours (4, 8, 12…) Make an X on these squares with a second color.
- Skip Count by eights (8, 16, 24…) Draw a box around these squares with a third color.

Complete the table.

	x2	x4	x8
1	2	4	8
2	4	8	16
3	6	12	24
4	8	16	32
5	10	20	40
6	12	24	48
7	14	28	56
8	16	32	64
9	18	36	72
10	20	40	80

Examine the table. Explain what you notice. **The products double each time.**

Page 77

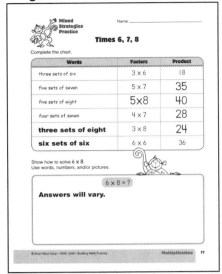

Mixed Strategies Practice

Times 6, 7, 8

Complete the chart.

Words	Factors	Product
three sets of six	3×6	18
five sets of seven	5×7	35
five sets of eight	5×8	40
four sets of seven	4×7	28
three sets of eight	3×8	24
six sets of six	6×6	36

Show how to solve 6×8. Use words, numbers, and/or pictures.

$6 \times 8 = ?$

Answers will vary.

Page 78

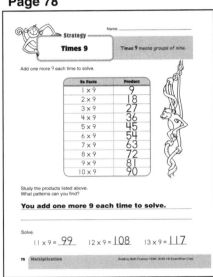

Strategy: **Times 9** — Times 9 means groups of nine.

Add one more 9 each time to solve.

9s Facts	Product
1×9	9
2×9	18
3×9	27
4×9	36
5×9	45
6×9	54
7×9	63
8×9	72
9×9	81
10×9	90

Study the products listed above. What patterns can you find?

You add one more 9 each time to solve.

Solve.

$11 \times 9 = 99$ $12 \times 9 = 108$ $13 \times 9 = 117$

Page 79

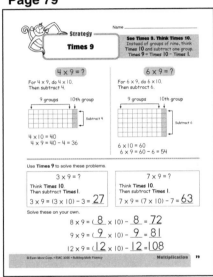

Strategy: **Times 9** — See Times 9. Think Times 10. Instead of groups of nine, think Times 10 and subtract one group. Times 9 = Times 10 – Times 1.

$4 \times 9 = ?$
For 4×9, do 4×10. Then subtract 4.

9 groups | 10th group — Subtract 4

$4 \times 10 = 40$
$4 \times 9 = 40 - 4 = 36$

$6 \times 9 = ?$
For 6×9, do 6×10. Then subtract 6.

9 groups | 10th group — Subtract 6

$6 \times 10 = 60$
$6 \times 9 = 60 - 6 = 54$

Use **Times 9** to solve these problems.

$3 \times 9 = ?$
Think Times 10. Then subtract Times 1.
$3 \times 9 = (3 \times 10) - 3 = 27$

$7 \times 9 = ?$
Think Times 10. Then subtract Times 1.
$7 \times 9 = (7 \times 10) - 7 = 63$

Solve these on your own.

$8 \times 9 = (8 \times 10) - 8 = 72$
$9 \times 9 = (9 \times 10) - 9 = 81$
$12 \times 9 = (12 \times 10) - 12 = 108$

Page 80

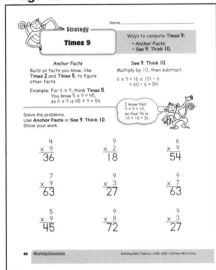

Strategy: **Times 9** — Ways to compute Times 9:
- Anchor Facts
- See Times 10.

Anchor Facts
Build on facts you know, like **Times 2** and **Times 5**, to figure other facts.

Example: For 6×9, think **Times 5**. You know $5 \times 9 = 45$, so 6×9 is $45 + 9 = 54$.

See 9. Think 10.
Multiply by 10, then subtract.
$6 \times 9 = (6 \times 10) - 6 = 60 - 6 = 54$

Solve the problems. Use **Anchor Facts** or **See 9. Think 10.** Show your work.

I know that $9 + 9 = 18$, so four 9s is $18 + 18 = 36$.

$\begin{array}{c}4\\\times 9\\\hline 36\end{array}$ $\begin{array}{c}9\\\times 2\\\hline 18\end{array}$ $\begin{array}{c}6\\\times 9\\\hline 54\end{array}$

$\begin{array}{c}7\\\times 9\\\hline 63\end{array}$ $\begin{array}{c}9\\\times 3\\\hline 27\end{array}$ $\begin{array}{c}9\\\times 7\\\hline 63\end{array}$

$\begin{array}{c}5\\\times 9\\\hline 45\end{array}$ $\begin{array}{c}9\\\times 8\\\hline 72\end{array}$ $\begin{array}{c}9\\\times 3\\\hline 27\end{array}$

Page 81

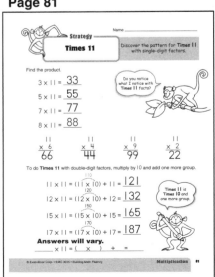

Strategy: **Times 11** — Discover the pattern for Times 11 with single-digit factors.

Find the product.

$3 \times 11 = 33$
$5 \times 11 = 55$
$7 \times 11 = 77$
$8 \times 11 = 88$

Do you notice what I notice with Times 11 facts?

$\begin{array}{c}11\\\times 6\\\hline 66\end{array}$ $\begin{array}{c}11\\\times 4\\\hline 44\end{array}$ $\begin{array}{c}11\\\times 9\\\hline 99\end{array}$ $\begin{array}{c}11\\\times 2\\\hline 22\end{array}$

To do Times 11 with double-digit factors, multiply by 10 and add one more group.

$11 \times 11 = (11 \times 10) + 11 = 121$
$12 \times 11 = (12 \times 10) + 12 = 132$
$15 \times 11 = (15 \times 10) + 15 = 165$
$17 \times 11 = (17 \times 10) + 17 = 187$

Times 11 is Times 10 and one more group.

Answers will vary.
___ $\times 11 = ($ ___ $) +$ ___ $=$ ___

Page 82

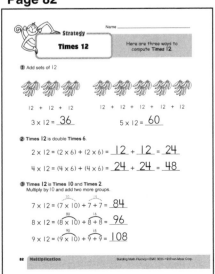

Strategy: **Times 12** — Here are three ways to compute Times 12.

① Add sets of 12

$12 + 12 + 12$
$3 \times 12 = 36$

$12 + 12 + 12 + 12 + 12$
$5 \times 12 = 60$

② Times 12 is double Times 6.

$2 \times 12 = (2 \times 6) + (2 \times 6) = 12 + 12 = 24$
$4 \times 12 = (4 \times 6) + (4 \times 6) = 24 + 24 = 48$

③ Times 12 is Times 10 and Times 2. Multiply by 10 and add two more groups.

$7 \times 12 = (7 \times 10) + 7 + 7 = 84$
$8 \times 12 = (8 \times 10) + 8 + 8 = 96$
$9 \times 12 = (9 \times 10) + 9 + 9 = 108$

Page 83

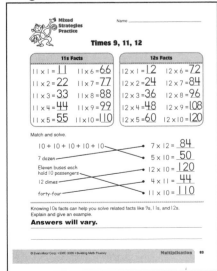

Mixed Strategies Practice

Times 9, 11, 12

11s Facts		12s Facts	
$11 \times 1 = 11$	$11 \times 6 = 66$	$12 \times 1 = 12$	$12 \times 6 = 72$
$11 \times 2 = 22$	$11 \times 7 = 77$	$12 \times 2 = 24$	$12 \times 7 = 84$
$11 \times 3 = 33$	$11 \times 8 = 88$	$12 \times 3 = 36$	$12 \times 8 = 96$
$11 \times 4 = 44$	$11 \times 9 = 99$	$12 \times 4 = 48$	$12 \times 9 = 108$
$11 \times 5 = 55$	$11 \times 10 = 110$	$12 \times 5 = 60$	$12 \times 10 = 120$

Match and solve.

$10 + 10 + 10 + 10 + 10$ • • $7 \times 12 = 84$
7 dozen • • $5 \times 10 = 50$
Eleven buses each hold 10 passengers • • $12 \times 10 = 120$
12 dimes • • $4 \times 11 = 44$
forty-four • • $11 \times 10 = 110$

Knowing 10s facts can help you solve related facts like 9s, 11s, and 12s. Explain and give an example.
Answers will vary.

Page 84

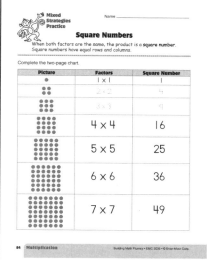

Mixed Strategies Practice

Square Numbers

When both factors are the same, the product is a **square number**.
Square numbers have equal rows and columns.

Complete the two-page chart.

Picture	Factors	Square Number
•	1 × 1	1
••	2 × 2	4
•••	3 × 3	9
••••	4 × 4	16
•••••	5 × 5	25
••••••	6 × 6	36
•••••••	7 × 7	49

84 Multiplication   Building Math Fluency • EMC 3035 • © Evan-Moor Corp.

Page 85

Mixed Strategies Practice

Square Numbers (continued)

Picture	Factors	Square Number
••••••••	8 × 8	64
•••••••••	9 × 9	81
••••••••••	10 × 10	100

Complete the list of square numbers.

1, 4, 9, 16, 25, 36, 49, 64, 81, 100

Examine your list for patterns, and record what you notice.

The factors that make a square number are the same.

© Evan-Moor Corp. • EMC 3035 • Building Math Fluency   Multiplication 85

Page 86

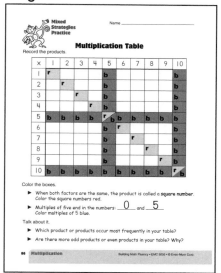

Mixed Strategies Practice

Multiplication Table

Record the products.

x	1	2	3	4	5	6	7	8	9	10
1	r				b					b
2		r			b					b
3			r		b					b
4				r	b					b
5	b	b	b	b		b	b	b	b	b
6					b					b
7					b		r			b
8					b					b
9					b				r	b
10	b	b	b	b	b	b	b	b	b	

Color the boxes.

► When both factors are the same, the product is called a **square number**. Color the square numbers red.

► Multiples of five end in the numbers: ___0___ and ___5___. Color multiples of 5 blue.

Talk about it.

► Which product or products occur most frequently in your table?

► Are there more odd products or even products in your table? Why?

86 Multiplication   Building Math Fluency • EMC 3035 • © Evan-Moor Corp.

Page 89

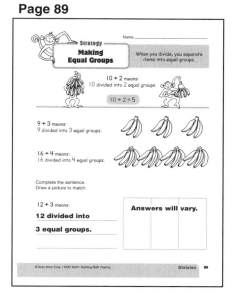

Strategy

Making Equal Groups — When you divide, you separate items into equal groups.

10 ÷ 2 means:
10 divided into 2 equal groups.

10 ÷ 2 = 5

9 ÷ 3 means:
9 divided into 3 equal groups.

16 ÷ 4 means:
16 divided into 4 equal groups.

Complete the sentence. Draw a picture to match.

12 ÷ 3 means:

12 divided into

3 equal groups.

Answers will vary.

© Evan-Moor Corp. • EMC 3035 • Building Math Fluency   Division 89

Page 90

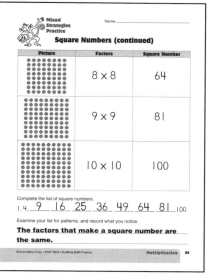

Strategy

Division of 0 — Division of 0 is always 0. If there are 0 items, there is nothing to divide into groups.

Divide.

0 ÷ 6 = 0   0 ÷ 3 = 0   0 ÷ 5 = 0

0 ÷ 7 = 0   0 ÷ 84 = 0   0 ÷ __ Answers will vary = 0

Division of 0 is not possible. 5 ÷ 0 can't be done.
How could you divide 5 items into 0 groups? It makes no sense.

Strategy

Division by 1 — A number divided by 1 equals the number.

If there are 3 bananas and 1 monkey, the monkey gets 3 bananas.
3 ÷ 1 = 3

If there are 6 bananas and 1 monkey, the monkey gets 6 bananas.
6 ÷ 1 = 6

Divide.

7 ÷ 1 = 7   9 ÷ 1 = 9   4 ÷ 1 = 4

5 ÷ 1 = 5   15 ÷ 1 = 15   8 ÷ 1 = 8

90 Division   Building Math Fluency • EMC 3035 • © Evan-Moor Corp.

Page 91

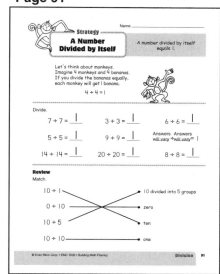

Strategy

A Number Divided by Itself — A number divided by itself equals 1.

Let's think about monkeys. Imagine 4 monkeys and 4 bananas. If you divide the bananas equally, each monkey will get 1 banana.

4 ÷ 4 = 1

Divide.

7 ÷ 7 = 1   3 ÷ 3 = 1   6 ÷ 6 = 1

5 ÷ 5 = 1   9 ÷ 9 = 1   Answers will vary = 1

14 ÷ 14 = 1   20 ÷ 20 = 1   8 ÷ 8 = 1

Review

Match.

10 ÷ 1 —— 10 divided into 5 groups
0 ÷ 10 —— zero
10 ÷ 5 —— ten
10 ÷ 10 —— one

© Evan-Moor Corp. • EMC 3035 • Building Math Fluency   Division 91

Page 92

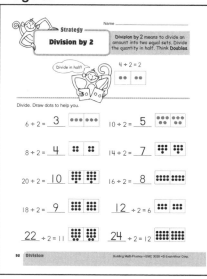

Strategy

Division by 2 — Division by 2 means to divide an amount into two equal sets. Divide the quantity in half. Think Doubles.

Divide in half!   4 ÷ 2 = 2

Divide. Draw dots to help you.

6 ÷ 2 = 3   10 ÷ 2 = 5

8 ÷ 2 = 4   14 ÷ 2 = 7

20 ÷ 2 = 10   16 ÷ 2 = 8

18 ÷ 2 = 9   12 ÷ 2 = 6

22 ÷ 2 = 11   24 ÷ 2 = 12

92 Division   Building Math Fluency • EMC 3035 • © Evan-Moor Corp.

Page 93

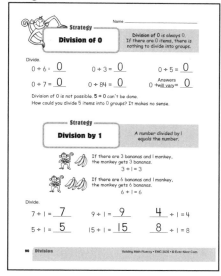

Strategy

Division by 3 — When you divide by 3, you are distributing items into three equal groups.

Imagine you are playing cards with two friends. All three of you need the same number of cards. The game has 18 cards. You deal them out one at a time.

Three Equal Groups

18 ÷ 3 = 6

Use tally marks to make three equal groups. Complete the equation.

12 ÷ 3 = 4

15 ÷ 3 = 5

18 ÷ 3 = 6

24 ÷ 3 = 8

27 ÷ 3 = 9

30 ÷ 3 = 10

© Evan-Moor Corp. • EMC 3035 • Building Math Fluency   Division 93

Page 94

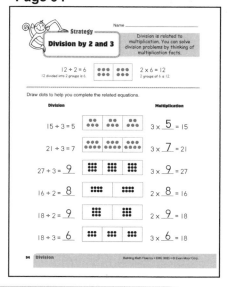

Strategy

Division by 2 and 3 — Division is related to multiplication. You can solve division problems by thinking of multiplication facts.

12 ÷ 2 = 6
12 divided into 2 groups is 6.

2 × 6 = 12
2 groups of 6 is 12.

Draw dots to help you complete the related equations.

Division		Multiplication
15 ÷ 3 = 5		3 × 5 = 15
21 ÷ 3 = 7		3 × 7 = 21
27 ÷ 3 = 9		3 × 9 = 27
16 ÷ 2 = 8		2 × 8 = 16
18 ÷ 2 = 9		2 × 9 = 18
18 ÷ 3 = 6		3 × 6 = 18

94 Division   Building Math Fluency • EMC 3035 • © Evan-Moor Corp.

© Evan-Moor Corp. • EMC 3035 • Building Math Fluency

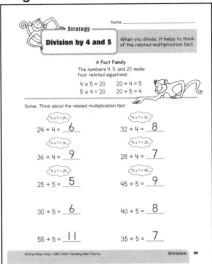

Strategy — Division by 4 and 5
When you divide, it helps to think of the related multiplication fact.

Name _____

A Fact Family
The numbers 4, 5, and 20 make four related equations:
$4 \times 5 = 20$ $20 \div 4 = 5$
$5 \times 4 = 20$ $20 \div 5 = 4$

Solve. Think about the related multiplication fact.

$24 \div 4 = 6$ ($4 \times ? = 24$) $32 \div 4 = 8$ ($4 \times ? = 32$)
$36 \div 4 = 9$ ($4 \times ? = 36$) $28 \div 4 = 7$ ($4 \times ? = 28$)
$25 \div 5 = 5$ ($5 \times ? = 25$) $45 \div 5 = 9$ ($5 \times ? = 45$)
$30 \div 5 = 6$ $40 \div 5 = 8$
$55 \div 5 = 11$ $35 \div 5 = 7$

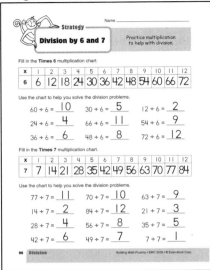

Strategy — Division by 6 and 7
Practice multiplication to help with division.

Name _____

Fill in the **Times 6** multiplication chart.

x	1	2	3	4	5	6	7	8	9	10	11	12
6	6	12	18	24	30	36	42	48	54	60	66	72

Use the chart to help you solve the division problems.
$60 \div 6 = 10$ $30 \div 6 = 5$ $12 \div 6 = 2$
$24 \div 6 = 4$ $66 \div 6 = 11$ $54 \div 6 = 9$
$36 \div 6 = 6$ $48 \div 6 = 8$ $72 \div 6 = 12$

Fill in the **Times 7** multiplication chart.

x	1	2	3	4	5	6	7	8	9	10	11	12
7	7	14	21	28	35	42	49	56	63	70	77	84

Use the chart to help you solve the division problems.
$77 \div 7 = 11$ $70 \div 7 = 10$ $63 \div 7 = 9$
$14 \div 7 = 2$ $84 \div 7 = 12$ $21 \div 7 = 3$
$28 \div 7 = 4$ $56 \div 7 = 8$ $35 \div 7 = 5$
$42 \div 7 = 6$ $49 \div 7 = 7$ $7 \div 7 = 1$

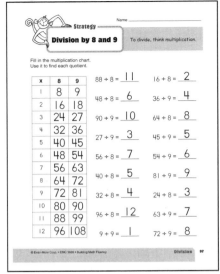

Strategy — Division by 8 and 9
To divide, think multiplication.

Name _____

Fill in the multiplication chart.
Use it to find each quotient.

x	8	9
1	8	9
2	16	18
3	24	27
4	32	36
5	40	45
6	48	54
7	56	63
8	64	72
9	72	81
10	80	90
11	88	99
12	96	108

$88 \div 8 = 11$ $16 \div 8 = 2$
$48 \div 8 = 6$ $36 \div 9 = 4$
$90 \div 9 = 10$ $64 \div 8 = 8$
$27 \div 9 = 3$ $45 \div 9 = 5$
$56 \div 8 = 7$ $54 \div 9 = 6$
$40 \div 8 = 5$ $81 \div 9 = 9$
$32 \div 8 = 4$ $24 \div 8 = 3$
$96 \div 8 = 12$ $63 \div 9 = 7$
$9 \div 9 = 1$ $72 \div 9 = 8$

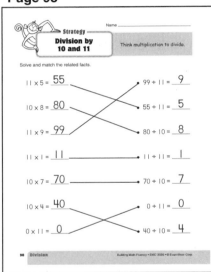

Strategy — Division by 10 and 11
Think multiplication to divide.

Name _____

Solve and match the related facts.

$11 \times 5 = 55$ → $99 \div 11 = 9$
$10 \times 8 = 80$ → $55 \div 11 = 5$
$11 \times 9 = 99$ → $80 \div 10 = 8$
$11 \times 1 = 11$ → $11 \div 11 = 1$
$10 \times 7 = 70$ → $70 \div 10 = 7$
$10 \times 4 = 40$ → $0 \div 11 = 0$
$0 \times 11 = 0$ → $40 \div 10 = 4$

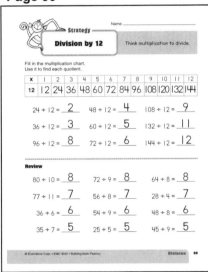

Strategy — Division by 12
Think multiplication to divide.

Name _____

Fill in the multiplication chart.
Use it to find each quotient.

x	1	2	3	4	5	6	7	8	9	10	11	12
12	12	24	36	48	60	72	84	96	108	120	132	144

$24 \div 12 = 2$ $48 \div 12 = 4$ $108 \div 12 = 9$
$36 \div 12 = 3$ $60 \div 12 = 5$ $132 \div 12 = 11$
$96 \div 12 = 8$ $72 \div 12 = 6$ $144 \div 12 = 12$

Review
$80 \div 10 = 8$ $72 \div 9 = 8$ $64 \div 8 = 8$
$77 \div 11 = 7$ $56 \div 8 = 7$ $28 \div 4 = 7$
$36 \div 6 = 6$ $54 \div 9 = 6$ $48 \div 8 = 6$
$35 \div 7 = 5$ $25 \div 5 = 5$ $45 \div 9 = 5$

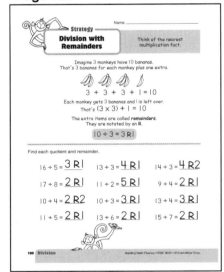

Strategy — Division with Remainders
Think of the nearest multiplication fact.

Name _____

Imagine 3 monkeys have 10 bananas.
That's 3 bananas for each monkey plus one extra.

$3 + 3 + 3 + 1 = 10$

Each monkey gets 3 bananas and 1 is left over.
That's $(3 \times 3) + 1 = 10$

The extra items are called **remainders**.
They are notated by an **R**.

$10 \div 3 = 3\ R1$

Find each quotient and remainder.
$16 \div 5 = 3\ R1$ $13 \div 3 = 4\ R1$ $14 \div 3 = 4\ R2$
$17 \div 8 = 2\ R1$ $11 \div 2 = 5\ R1$ $9 \div 4 = 2\ R1$
$10 \div 4 = 2\ R2$ $10 \div 3 = 3\ R1$ $13 \div 4 = 3\ R1$
$11 \div 5 = 2\ R1$ $13 \div 6 = 2\ R1$ $15 \div 7 = 2\ R1$

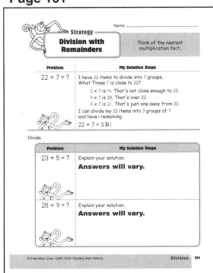

Strategy — Division with Remainders
Think of the nearest multiplication fact.

Name _____

Problem	My Solution Steps
$22 \div 7 = ?$	I have 22 items to divide into 7 groups. What Times 7 is close to 22? 2×7 is 14. That's not close enough to 22. 4×7 is 28. That's over 22. 3×7 is 21. That's just one away from 22. I can divide my 22 items into 3 groups of 7 and have 1 remaining. $22 \div 7 = 3\ R1$

Divide.

Problem	My Solution Steps
$23 \div 5 = ?$	Explain your solution. **Answers will vary.**
$28 \div 9 = ?$	Explain your solution. **Answers will vary.**

Sums 0 to 10   Name _____   My Score _____

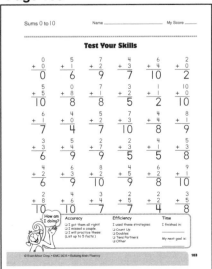

Test Your Skills

0 + 0 = 0	5 + 1 = 6	7 + 2 = 9	4 + 3 = 7	6 + 4 = 10	2 + 0 = 2
5 + 5 = 10	0 + 8 = 8	7 + 1 = 8	3 + 2 = 5	1 + 1 = 2	10 + 0 = 10
6 + 1 = 7	4 + 0 = 4	5 + 2 = 7	7 + 3 = 10	4 + 4 = 8	8 + 1 = 9
3 + 3 = 6	5 + 4 = 9	2 + 7 = 9	2 + 3 = 5	4 + 1 = 5	5 + 3 = 8
4 + 2 = 6	6 + 3 = 9	8 + 2 = 10	4 + 5 = 9	6 + 2 = 8	9 + 1 = 10
2 + 8 = 10	4 + 6 = ?	3 + 4 = 7	5 + 2 = ?	2 + 2 = ?	3 + 5 = 8

How am I doing?
Accuracy: ☐ I got them all right! ☐ I missed a couple. ☐ I will practice these: (List up to 5 facts.)
Efficiency: I used these strategies: ☐ Count Up ☐ Doubles ☐ Ten Partners ☐ Other
Time: I finished in: _____ My next goal is: _____

Sums 11 to 15
Test 1   Name _____   My Score _____

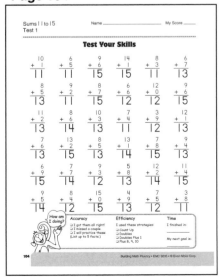

Test Your Skills

10 + 1 = 11	6 + 5 = 11	9 + 6 = 15	14 + 1 = 15	8 + 3 = 11	6 + 7 = 13
8 + 5 = 13	9 + 2 = 11	8 + 7 = 15	6 + 6 = 12	12 + 0 = 12	9 + 6 = 15
11 + 2 = 13	8 + 6 = 14	10 + 3 = 13	7 + 4 = 11	3 + 9 = 12	12 + 1 = 13
7 + 6 = 13	13 + 2 = 15	8 + 5 = 13	6 + 8 = 14	7 + 8 = 15	9 + 4 = 13
6 + 9 = 15	7 + 7 = 14	3 + 9 = 12	5 + 8 = 13	8 + 6 = 14	11 + 4 = 15
9 + 5 = 14	8 + 6 = 14	12 + 0 = 12	4 + 9 = 13	7 + 5 = 12	3 + 9 = 12

How am I doing?
Accuracy: ☐ I got them all right! ☐ I missed a couple. ☐ I will practice these: (List up to 5 facts.)
Efficiency: I used these strategies: ☐ Count Up ☐ Doubles ☐ Doubles Plus 1 ☐ Plus 8, 9, 10
Time: I finished in: _____ My next goal is: _____

Page 105

Sums 11 to 15
Test 2

Test Your Skills

10 + 5 = 15	9 + 3 = 12	6 + 6 = 12	11 + 1 = 12	7 + 5 = 12	2 + 9 = 11
5 + 9 = 14	7 + 4 = 11	12 + 3 = 15	9 + 5 = 14	8 + 6 = 14	4 + 8 = 12
11 + 0 = 11	6 + 8 = 14	7 + 6 = 13	8 + 4 = 12	5 + 7 = 12	6 + 9 = 15
9 + 4 = 13	14 + 0 = 14	8 + 7 = 15	9 + 6 = 15	6 + 5 = 11	8 + 6 = 14
14 + 1 = 15	9 + 2 = 11	10 + 4 = 14	8 + 5 = 13	11 + 3 = 14	4 + 7 = 11
5 + 6 = 11	8 + 3 = 11	7 + 8 = 15	2 + 10 = 12	5 + 9 = 14	9 + 6 = 15

How am I doing?

Accuracy: I got them all right! / I missed a couple. / I will practice these: (List up to 5 facts.)
Efficiency — I used these strategies: Count Up / Doubles / Doubles Plus 1 / Plus 8, 9, 10
Time — I finished in:

© Evan-Moor Corp. • EMC 3035 • Building Math Fluency   105

Page 106

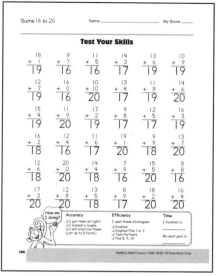

Sums 16 to 20

Test Your Skills

18 + 1 = 19	9 + 7 = 16	11 + 5 = 16	14 + 3 = 17	13 + 6 = 19	10 + 9 = 19
12 + 7 = 19	16 + 0 = 16	10 + 10 = 20	13 + 4 = 17	11 + 8 = 19	14 + 6 = 20
15 + 4 = 19	9 + 7 = 16	17 + 2 = 19	9 + 8 = 17	12 + 5 = 17	16 + 3 = 19
16 + 2 = 18	12 + 4 = 16	11 + 6 = 17	19 + 1 = 20	9 + 9 = 18	13 + 7 = 20
12 + 6 = 18	20 + 0 = 20	14 + 4 = 18	9 + 9 = 18	15 + 5 = 20	8 + 8 = 16
17 + 3 = 20	12 + 6 = 18	13 + 5 = 18	8 + 9 = 17	18 + 2 = 20	16 + 4 = 20

How am I doing?

Accuracy: I got them all right! / I missed a couple. / I will practice these: (List up to 5 facts.)
Efficiency — I used these strategies: Doubles / Doubles Plus 1 or 2 / Tens Partners / Plus 8, 9, 10
Time — I finished in:

106   © Evan-Moor Corp. • EMC 3035 • Building Math Fluency

Page 107

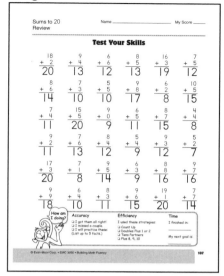

Sums to 20
Review

Test Your Skills

18 + 2 = 20	9 + 4 = 13	6 + 6 = 12	8 + 5 = 13	16 + 3 = 19	7 + 5 = 12
8 + 6 = 14	7 + 3 = 10	5 + 5 = 10	8 + 0 = 8	6 + 2 = 8	10 + 5 = 15
7 + 4 = 11	15 + 5 = 20	9 + 0 = 9	6 + 1 = 7	7 + 8 = 15	4 + 4 = 8
9 + 4 = 13	7 + 5 = 12	8 + 4 = 12	5 + 4 = 9	5 + 7 = 12	5 + 2 = 7
17 + 3 = 20	7 + 1 = 8	9 + 5 = 14	6 + 3 = 9	8 + 8 = 16	9 + 7 = 16
9 + 9 = 18	2 + 8 = 10	8 + 7 = 15	9 + 11 = 20	19 + 7 = ...	7 + 7 = 14

How am I doing?

Accuracy: I got them all right! / I missed a couple. / I will practice these: (List up to 5 facts.)
Efficiency — I used these strategies: Count Back 1, 2, or 3 / Count Up from bottom number / Tens Partners / Plus 8, 9, 10
Time — I finished in:

© Evan-Moor Corp. • EMC 3035 • Building Math Fluency   107

Page 108

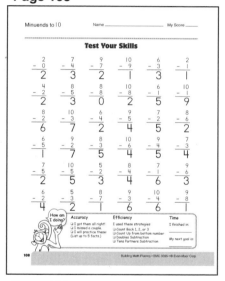

Minuends to 10

Test Your Skills

2 − 0 = 2	7 − 4 = 3	9 − 7 = 2	10 − 9 = 1	6 − 3 = 3	2 − 1 = 1
4 − 2 = 2	8 − 5 = 3	8 − 8 = 0	10 − 8 = 2	6 − 1 = 5	10 − 1 = 9
8 − 2 = 6	10 − 3 = 7	6 − 4 = 2	9 − 5 = 4	7 − 2 = 5	8 − 6 = 2
6 − 5 = 1	9 − 2 = 7	8 − 3 = 5	10 − 6 = 4	9 − 4 = 5	7 − 3 = 4
7 − 5 = 2	10 − 5 = 5	5 − 1 = 4	8 − 4 = 4	7 − 1 = 6	9 − 6 = 3
6 − 4 = 2	5 − 3 = 2	8 − 7 = 1	9 − 3 = 6	10 − 4 = ...	9 − 8 = ...

How am I doing?

Accuracy: I got them all right! / I missed a couple. / I will practice these: (List up to 5 facts.)
Efficiency — I used these strategies: Count Back 1, 2, or 3 / Doubles Subtraction / Tens Partners Subtraction
Time — I finished in:

108   Building Math Fluency • EMC 3035 • © Evan-Moor Corp.

Page 109

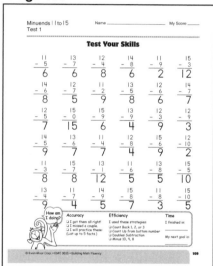

Minuends 11 to 15
Test 1

Test Your Skills

11 − 5 = 6	13 − 7 = 6	12 − 4 = 8	14 − 8 = 6	11 − 9 = 2	15 − 3 = 12
14 − 6 = 8	12 − 7 = 5	11 − 2 = 9	13 − 5 = 8	12 − 6 = 6	14 − 7 = 7
12 − 5 = 7	15 − 0 = 15	15 − 9 = 6	13 − 9 = 4	12 − 3 = 9	12 − 9 = 3
14 − 5 = 9	13 − 6 = 7	11 − 4 = 7	12 − 8 = 4	15 − 6 = 9	12 − 10 = 2
11 − 3 = 8	15 − 7 = 8	13 − 1 = 12	11 − 6 = 5	13 − 8 = 5	15 − 5 = 10
13 − 4 = ...	11 − 7 = ...	14 − 9 = ...	15 − 8 = ...	11 − 8 = ...	15 − 10 = 5

How am I doing?

Accuracy: I got them all right! / I missed a couple. / I will practice these: (List up to 5 facts.)
Efficiency — I used these strategies: Count Back 1, 2, or 3 / Count Up from bottom number / Doubles Subtraction / Minus 10, 9, 8
Time — I finished in:

© Evan-Moor Corp. • EMC 3035 • Building Math Fluency   109

Page 110

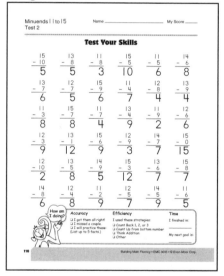

Minuends 11 to 15
Test 2

Test Your Skills

15 − 10 = 5	13 − 8 = 5	11 − 8 = 3	15 − 5 = 10	11 − 5 = 6	14 − 6 = 8
13 − 7 = 6	12 − 7 = 5	15 − 4 = 11	11 − 4 = 7	13 − 9 = 4	12 − 8 = 4
11 − 3 = 8	15 − 7 = 8	11 − 7 = 4	13 − 4 = 9	11 − 9 = 2	12 − 6 = 6
12 − 3 = 9	13 − 1 = 12	15 − 6 = 9	12 − 9 = 3	14 − 7 = 7	15 − 0 = 15
12 − 10 = 2	13 − 5 = 8	14 − 9 = 5	15 − 3 = 12	13 − 6 = 7	15 − 8 = 7
14 − 8 = 6	12 − 4 = 8	11 − 2 = 9	12 − 5 = 7	14 − 5 = 9	11 − 6 = 5

How am I doing?

Accuracy: I got them all right! / I missed a couple. / I will practice these: (List up to 5 facts.)
Efficiency — I used these strategies: Count Back 1, 2, or 3 / Count Up from bottom number / Think Addition / Other
Time — I finished in:

110   Building Math Fluency • EMC 3035 • © Evan-Moor Corp.

Page 111

Minuends 16 to 20

Test Your Skills

17 − 2 = 15	20 − 10 = 10	16 − 9 = 7	18 − 9 = 9	20 − 8 = 12	16 − 0 = 16
20 − 5 = 15	16 − 8 = 8	19 − 0 = 19	17 − 6 = 11	20 − 15 = 5	16 − 6 = 10
19 − 5 = 14	17 − 3 = 14	20 − 18 = 2	16 − 9 = 7	17 − 14 = 3	20 − 7 = 13
20 − 1 = 19	18 − 8 = 10	17 − 8 = 9	19 − 6 = 13	20 − 3 = 17	18 − 5 = 13
20 − 10 = 7	16 − 7 = 9	16 − 2 = 14	20 − 4 = 16	17 − 9 = 8	18 − 7 = 11
18 − 6 = ...	17 − 8 = ...	20 − 9 = ...	16 − 7 = ...	19 − 4 = ...	20 − 20 = 0

How am I doing?

Accuracy: I got them all right! / I missed a couple. / I will practice these: (List up to 5 facts.)
Efficiency — I used these strategies: Count Back 1, 2, or 3 / Count Up from bottom number / Think Addition / Other
Time — I finished in:

© Evan-Moor Corp. • EMC 3035 • Building Math Fluency   111

Page 112

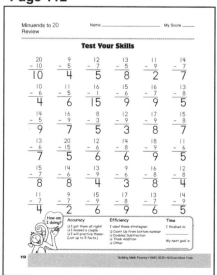

Minuends to 20
Review

Test Your Skills

20 − 10 = 10	9 − 5 = 4	12 − 7 = 5	13 − 5 = 8	11 − 9 = 2	14 − 7 = 7
10 − 6 = 4	11 − 5 = 6	16 − 1 = 15	15 − 6 = 9	16 − 7 = 9	13 − 8 = 5
14 − 5 = 9	16 − 4 = 16	8 − 5 = 3	12 − 4 = 8	17 − 9 = 8	15 − 8 = 7
13 − 6 = 7	20 − 6 = 5	12 − 6 = 6	14 − 8 = 6	18 − 9 = 9	11 − 6 = 5
15 − 7 = 8	14 − 6 = 8	13 − 9 = 4	9 − 6 = 3	16 − 8 = 8	12 − 8 = 4
11 − 7 = 4	9 − 2 = 7	15 − 9 = 6	17 − 9 = 8	13 − 9 = 4	14 − 9 = ...

How am I doing?

Accuracy: I got them all right! / I missed a couple. / I will practice these: (List up to 5 facts.)
Efficiency — I used these strategies: Count Up from bottom number / Doubles Subtraction / Think Addition / Other
Time — I finished in:

112   Building Math Fluency • EMC 3035 • © Evan-Moor Corp.

Page 113

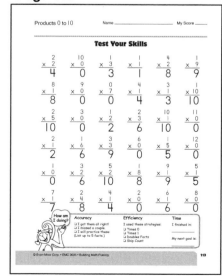

Products 0 to 10

Test Your Skills

2 × 2 = 4	10 × 0 = 0	1 × 3 = 3	1 × 1 = 1	4 × 2 = 8	1 × 9 = 9
8 × 1 = 8	9 × 0 = 0	0 × 7 = 0	4 × 1 = 4	3 × 1 = 3	1 × 10 = 10
2 × 5 = 10	0 × 1 = 0	1 × 2 = 2	2 × 3 = 6	10 × 1 = 10	11 × 0 = 0
2 × 1 = 2	6 × 1 = 6	3 × 3 = 9	0 × 1 = 0	5 × 1 = 5	12 × 0 = 0
0 × 0 = 0	3 × 2 = 6	10 × 1 = 10	8 × 1 = 5	5 × 1 = 5	1 × 5 = 5
7 × 1 = 7	2 × 4 = ...	4 × 1 = ...	2 × 2 = ...	6 × 0 = ...	8 × 0 = ...

How am I doing?

Accuracy: I got them all right! / I missed a couple. / I will practice these: (List up to 5 facts.)
Efficiency — I used these strategies: Times 0 / Times 1 / Double Facts / Skip Count
Time — I finished in:

© Evan-Moor Corp. • EMC 3035 • Building Math Fluency   113

Page 114
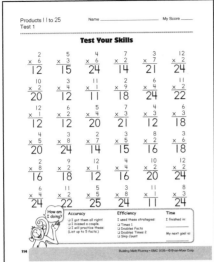

Page 115

Page 116
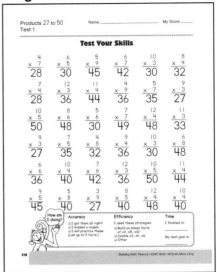

Page 117
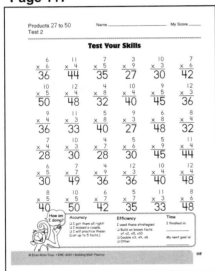

Page 118

Page 119

Page 120
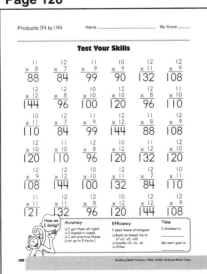

Page 121
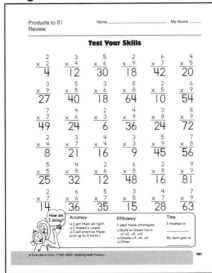

Page 122
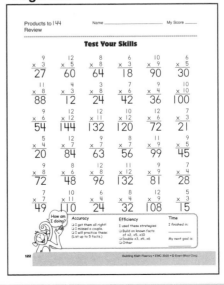

Dividends 0 to 10 Name _____ My Score _____

Test Your Skills

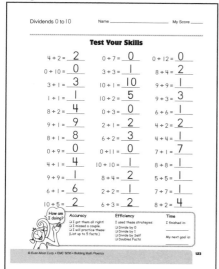

4 ÷ 2 = 2	0 ÷ 7 = 0	0 ÷ 12 = 0
0 ÷ 10 = 0	3 ÷ 3 = 1	8 ÷ 4 = 2
3 ÷ 1 = 3	10 ÷ 1 = 10	9 ÷ 9 = 1
1 ÷ 1 = 1	10 ÷ 2 = 5	9 ÷ 3 = 3
8 ÷ 2 = 4	0 ÷ 3 = 0	6 ÷ 6 = 1
9 ÷ 1 = 9	2 ÷ 1 = 2	4 ÷ 2 = 2
8 ÷ 1 = 8	6 ÷ 2 = 3	4 ÷ 4 = 1
0 ÷ 9 = 0	0 ÷ 11 = 0	7 ÷ 1 = 7
4 ÷ 1 = 4	10 ÷ 10 = 1	8 ÷ 8 = 1
9 ÷ 9 = 1	8 ÷ 4 = 2	5 ÷ 5 = 1
6 ÷ 1 = 6	2 ÷ 2 = 1	7 ÷ 7 = 1
10 ÷ 5 = 2	6 ÷ 3 = 2	8 ÷ 2 = 4

How am I doing? Accuracy · Efficiency · Time

Dividends 11 to 25 — Test 1 Name _____ My Score _____

Test Your Skills

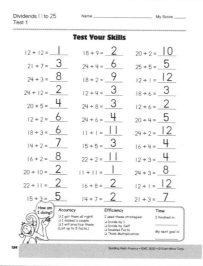

12 ÷ 12 = 1	18 ÷ 9 = 2	20 ÷ 2 = 10
21 ÷ 7 = 3	24 ÷ 4 = 6	25 ÷ 5 = 5
24 ÷ 3 = 8	18 ÷ 2 = 9	12 ÷ 1 = 12
24 ÷ 12 = 2	12 ÷ 4 = 3	18 ÷ 6 = 3
20 ÷ 5 = 4	24 ÷ 8 = 3	12 ÷ 2 = 2
12 ÷ 2 = 6	24 ÷ 6 = 4	20 ÷ 4 = 5
18 ÷ 3 = 6	11 ÷ 1 = 11	24 ÷ 2 = 12
14 ÷ 2 = 7	15 ÷ 5 = 3	16 ÷ 4 = 4
16 ÷ 2 = 8	22 ÷ 11 = 2	12 ÷ 3 = 4
20 ÷ 5 = 2	11 ÷ 11 = 1	24 ÷ 3 = 8
22 ÷ 11 = 2	16 ÷ 8 = 2	12 ÷ 1 = 12
15 ÷ 3 = 5	14 ÷ 7 = 2	21 ÷ 3 = 7

How am I doing? Accuracy · Efficiency · Time

Dividends 11 to 25 — Test 2 Name _____ My Score _____

Test Your Skills

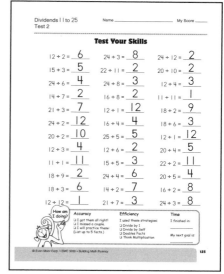

12 ÷ 2 = 6	24 ÷ 3 = 8	24 ÷ 12 = 2
15 ÷ 3 = 5	22 ÷ 11 = 2	20 ÷ 10 = 2
24 ÷ 6 = 4	24 ÷ 8 = 3	12 ÷ 4 = 3
14 ÷ 7 = 2	16 ÷ 2 = 8	11 ÷ 1 = 11
21 ÷ 3 = 7	12 ÷ 1 = 12	18 ÷ 2 = 9
24 ÷ 2 = 12	16 ÷ 4 = 4	18 ÷ 6 = 3
20 ÷ 2 = 10	25 ÷ 5 = 5	12 ÷ 1 = 12
12 ÷ 3 = 4	12 ÷ 6 = 2	20 ÷ 4 = 5
11 ÷ 1 = 11	15 ÷ 5 = 3	22 ÷ 2 = 11
18 ÷ 9 = 2	24 ÷ 4 = 6	20 ÷ 5 = 4
18 ÷ 3 = 6	14 ÷ 2 = 7	16 ÷ 2 = 8
12 ÷ 12 = 1	21 ÷ 7 = 3	24 ÷ 3 = 8

How am I doing? Accuracy · Efficiency · Time

Dividends 27 to 50 — Test 1 Name _____ My Score _____

Test Your Skills

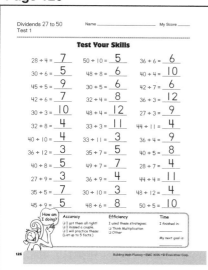

28 ÷ 4 = 7	50 ÷ 10 = 5	36 ÷ 6 = 6
30 ÷ 6 = 5	48 ÷ 8 = 6	40 ÷ 4 = 10
45 ÷ 5 = 9	30 ÷ 5 = 6	42 ÷ 7 = 6
42 ÷ 6 = 7	32 ÷ 4 = 8	36 ÷ 3 = 12
30 ÷ 3 = 10	48 ÷ 4 = 12	27 ÷ 3 = 9
32 ÷ 8 = 4	33 ÷ 3 = 11	44 ÷ 11 = 4
40 ÷ 10 = 4	33 ÷ 11 = 3	36 ÷ 4 = 9
36 ÷ 12 = 3	35 ÷ 7 = 5	40 ÷ 5 = 8
40 ÷ 8 = 5	49 ÷ 7 = 7	28 ÷ 7 = 4
27 ÷ 9 = 3	36 ÷ 9 = 4	44 ÷ 4 = 11
35 ÷ 5 = 7	30 ÷ 10 = 3	48 ÷ 12 = 4
45 ÷ 9 = 5	48 ÷ 8 = 6	50 ÷ 5 = 10

How am I doing? Accuracy · Efficiency · Time

Dividends 27 to 50 — Test 2 Name _____ My Score _____

Test Your Skills

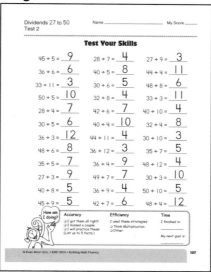

45 ÷ 5 = 9	28 ÷ 7 = 4	27 ÷ 9 = 3
36 ÷ 6 = 6	40 ÷ 5 = 8	44 ÷ 4 = 11
33 ÷ 11 = 3	30 ÷ 6 = 5	48 ÷ 8 = 6
50 ÷ 5 = 10	32 ÷ 8 = 4	33 ÷ 3 = 11
28 ÷ 4 = 7	42 ÷ 6 = 7	40 ÷ 10 = 4
30 ÷ 5 = 6	40 ÷ 4 = 10	32 ÷ 4 = 8
36 ÷ 3 = 12	44 ÷ 11 = 4	30 ÷ 10 = 3
48 ÷ 6 = 8	36 ÷ 12 = 3	35 ÷ 5 = 7
35 ÷ 5 = 7	36 ÷ 4 = 9	48 ÷ 12 = 4
27 ÷ 3 = 9	49 ÷ 7 = 7	30 ÷ 3 = 10
40 ÷ 8 = 5	36 ÷ 9 = 4	50 ÷ 10 = 5
45 ÷ 9 = 5	42 ÷ 7 = 6	48 ÷ 4 = 12

How am I doing? Accuracy · Efficiency · Time

Dividends 54 to 81 — Test 1 Name _____ My Score _____

Test Your Skills

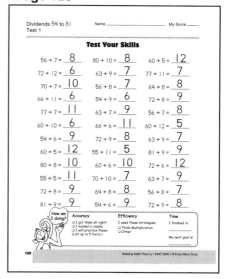

56 ÷ 7 = 8	80 ÷ 10 = 8	60 ÷ 5 = 12
72 ÷ 12 = 6	63 ÷ 9 = 7	77 ÷ 11 = 7
70 ÷ 7 = 10	56 ÷ 8 = 7	64 ÷ 8 = 8
66 ÷ 11 = 6	54 ÷ 9 = 6	72 ÷ 8 = 9
77 ÷ 7 = 11	63 ÷ 7 = 9	56 ÷ 7 = 8
60 ÷ 10 = 6	66 ÷ 6 = 11	60 ÷ 12 = 5
54 ÷ 6 = 9	72 ÷ 9 = 8	63 ÷ 9 = 7
60 ÷ 5 = 12	55 ÷ 11 = 5	81 ÷ 9 = 9
80 ÷ 8 = 10	60 ÷ 6 = 10	72 ÷ 6 = 12
55 ÷ 5 = 11	70 ÷ 10 = 7	63 ÷ 7 = 9
72 ÷ 8 = 9	64 ÷ 8 = 8	56 ÷ 8 = 7
81 ÷ 9 = 9	54 ÷ 6 = 9	72 ÷ 9 = 8

How am I doing? Accuracy · Efficiency · Time

Dividends 54 to 81 — Test 2 Name _____ My Score _____

Test Your Skills

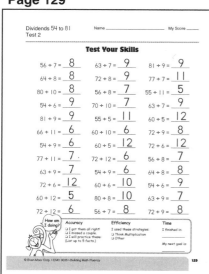

56 ÷ 7 = 8	63 ÷ 7 = 9	81 ÷ 9 = 9
64 ÷ 8 = 8	72 ÷ 8 = 9	77 ÷ 7 = 11
80 ÷ 10 = 8	56 ÷ 8 = 7	55 ÷ 11 = 5
54 ÷ 6 = 9	70 ÷ 10 = 7	63 ÷ 7 = 9
81 ÷ 9 = 9	55 ÷ 5 = 11	60 ÷ 5 = 12
66 ÷ 11 = 6	60 ÷ 10 = 6	72 ÷ 9 = 8
54 ÷ 9 = 6	60 ÷ 5 = 12	72 ÷ 6 = 12
77 ÷ 11 = 7	72 ÷ 12 = 6	56 ÷ 8 = 7
63 ÷ 9 = 7	54 ÷ 9 = 6	64 ÷ 8 = 8
72 ÷ 6 = 12	60 ÷ 6 = 10	54 ÷ 6 = 9
60 ÷ 12 = 5	80 ÷ 8 = 10	72 ÷ 8 = 9

How am I doing? Accuracy · Efficiency · Time

Dividends 84 to 144 Name _____ My Score _____

Test Your Skills

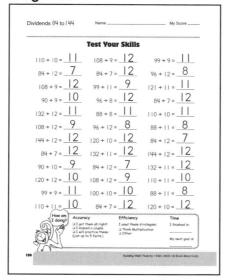

110 ÷ 10 = 11	108 ÷ 9 = 12	99 ÷ 9 = 11
84 ÷ 12 = 7	84 ÷ 7 = 12	96 ÷ 12 = 8
108 ÷ 9 = 12	99 ÷ 11 = 9	121 ÷ 11 = 11
90 ÷ 9 = 10	96 ÷ 8 = 12	84 ÷ 7 = 12
132 ÷ 12 = 11	88 ÷ 8 = 11	110 ÷ 10 = 11
108 ÷ 12 = 9	96 ÷ 12 = 8	88 ÷ 11 = 8
144 ÷ 12 = 12	120 ÷ 10 = 12	84 ÷ 12 = 7
84 ÷ 7 = 12	132 ÷ 11 = 12	144 ÷ 12 = 12
90 ÷ 10 = 9	84 ÷ 12 = 7	132 ÷ 12 = 11
120 ÷ 12 = 10	108 ÷ 12 = 9	110 ÷ 11 = 10
99 ÷ 9 = 11	100 ÷ 10 = 10	88 ÷ 11 = 8
110 ÷ 11 = 10	84 ÷ 7 = 12	120 ÷ 10 = 12

How am I doing? Accuracy · Efficiency · Time

Dividends to 81 — Review Name _____ My Score _____

Test Your Skills

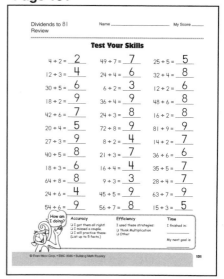

4 ÷ 2 = 2	49 ÷ 7 = 7	25 ÷ 5 = 5
12 ÷ 3 = 4	24 ÷ 4 = 6	32 ÷ 4 = 8
30 ÷ 5 = 6	6 ÷ 2 = 3	12 ÷ 2 = 6
18 ÷ 2 = 9	36 ÷ 4 = 9	48 ÷ 6 = 8
42 ÷ 6 = 7	24 ÷ 3 = 8	16 ÷ 2 = 8
20 ÷ 4 = 5	72 ÷ 8 = 9	81 ÷ 9 = 9
27 ÷ 3 = 9	8 ÷ 2 = 4	14 ÷ 2 = 7
40 ÷ 5 = 8	21 ÷ 3 = 7	36 ÷ 6 = 6
18 ÷ 3 = 6	16 ÷ 4 = 4	35 ÷ 5 = 7
64 ÷ 8 = 8	9 ÷ 3 = 3	28 ÷ 4 = 7
24 ÷ 6 = 4	45 ÷ 5 = 9	63 ÷ 7 = 9
54 ÷ 6 = 9	56 ÷ 7 = 8	15 ÷ 3 = 5

How am I doing? Accuracy · Efficiency · Time

Page 132

Dividends to 144
Review

Name _____ My Score _____

Test Your Skills

27 ÷ 9 = 3	54 ÷ 9 = 6	72 ÷ 9 = 8
60 ÷ 12 = 5	144 ÷ 12 = 12	40 ÷ 8 = 5
64 ÷ 8 = 8	132 ÷ 12 = 11	96 ÷ 12 = 8
18 ÷ 6 = 3	108 ÷ 9 = 12	132 ÷ 11 = 12
90 ÷ 10 = 9	72 ÷ 12 = 6	81 ÷ 9 = 9
30 ÷ 6 = 5	21 ÷ 7 = 3	28 ÷ 7 = 4
88 ÷ 11 = 8	20 ÷ 5 = 4	49 ÷ 7 = 7
12 ÷ 4 = 3	84 ÷ 12 = 7	110 ÷ 10 = 11
24 ÷ 8 = 3	63 ÷ 9 = 7	24 ÷ 6 = 4
42 ÷ 7 = 6	48 ÷ 8 = 6	32 ÷ 8 = 4
36 ÷ 9 = 4	99 ÷ 11 = 9	108 ÷ 12 = 9
100 ÷ 10 = 10	15 ÷ 5 = 3	36 ÷ 9 = 4

How am I doing?

Accuracy	Efficiency	Time
❑ I got them all right!	I used these strategies:	I finished in:
❑ I missed a couple.	❑ Think Multiplication	
❑ I will practice these:	❑ Other	
(List up to 5 facts.)		My next goal is:

Building Math Fluency • EMC 3035 • © Evan-Moor Corp.

Building Math Fluency • EMC 3035 • © Evan-Moor Corp.

Page 123

Dividends 0 to 10   Name _____   My Score ____

Test Your Skills

4 ÷ 2 = 2	0 ÷ 7 = 0	0 ÷ 12 = 0
0 ÷ 10 = 0	3 ÷ 3 = 1	8 ÷ 4 = 2
3 ÷ 1 = 3	10 ÷ 1 = 10	9 ÷ 9 = 1
1 ÷ 1 = 1	10 ÷ 2 = 5	9 ÷ 3 = 3
8 ÷ 2 = 4	0 ÷ 3 = 0	6 ÷ 6 = 1
9 ÷ 1 = 9	2 ÷ 1 = 2	4 ÷ 2 = 2
8 ÷ 1 = 8	6 ÷ 2 = 3	4 ÷ 4 = 1
0 ÷ 9 = 0	0 ÷ 11 = 0	7 ÷ 1 = 7
4 ÷ 1 = 4	10 ÷ 10 = 1	8 ÷ 8 = 1
9 ÷ 9 = 1	8 ÷ 4 = 2	5 ÷ 5 = 1
6 ÷ 1 = 6	2 ÷ 2 = 1	7 ÷ 7 = 1
10 ÷ 5 = 2	6 ÷ 3 = 2	8 ÷ 2 = 4

How am I doing? — Accuracy: I got them all right! / I missed a couple. / I will practice these: (List up to 5 facts.) — Efficiency: I used these strategies: Divide by 0 / Divide by 1 / Divide by Self / Doubles Facts — Time: I finished in: My next goal is:

123

Page 124

Dividends 11 to 25 Test 1   Name _____   My Score ____

Test Your Skills

12 ÷ 12 = 1	18 ÷ 9 = 2	20 ÷ 2 = 10
21 ÷ 7 = 3	24 ÷ 4 = 6	25 ÷ 5 = 5
24 ÷ 3 = 8	18 ÷ 2 = 9	12 ÷ 1 = 12
24 ÷ 12 = 2	12 ÷ 4 = 3	18 ÷ 6 = 3
20 ÷ 5 = 4	24 ÷ 8 = 3	12 ÷ 6 = 2
12 ÷ 2 = 6	24 ÷ 6 = 4	20 ÷ 4 = 5
18 ÷ 3 = 6	11 ÷ 1 = 11	24 ÷ 2 = 12
14 ÷ 2 = 7	15 ÷ 5 = 3	16 ÷ 4 = 4
16 ÷ 2 = 8	22 ÷ 11 = 11	12 ÷ 3 = 4
20 ÷ 10 = 2	11 ÷ 11 = 1	24 ÷ 3 = 8
22 ÷ 11 = 2	16 ÷ 8 = 2	12 ÷ 1 = 12
15 ÷ 3 = 5	14 ÷ 7 = 2	21 ÷ 3 = 7

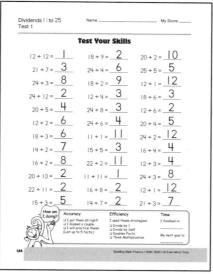

How am I doing? — Accuracy: I got them all right! / I missed a couple. / I will practice these: (List up to 5 facts.) — Efficiency: I used these strategies: Divide by 1 / Divide by Self / Doubles Facts / Think Multiplication — Time: I finished in: My next goal is:

124

Page 125

Dividends 11 to 25 Test 2   Name _____   My Score ____

Test Your Skills

12 ÷ 2 = 6	24 ÷ 3 = 8	24 ÷ 12 = 2
15 ÷ 3 = 4	22 ÷ 11 = 2	20 ÷ 10 = 2
24 ÷ 6 = 2	24 ÷ 8 = 2	12 ÷ 4 = 1
14 ÷ 7 = 2	16 ÷ 2 = 8	11 ÷ 11 = 1
21 ÷ 3 = 7	12 ÷ 1 = 12	18 ÷ 2 = 9
24 ÷ 2 = 12	16 ÷ 4 = 4	18 ÷ 6 = 3
20 ÷ 2 = 10	25 ÷ 5 = 5	12 ÷ 1 = 12
12 ÷ 3 = 4	12 ÷ 6 = 2	20 ÷ 4 = 5
11 ÷ 1 = 11	15 ÷ 5 = 3	22 ÷ 2 = 11
18 ÷ 9 = 2	24 ÷ 4 = 6	20 ÷ 5 = 4
18 ÷ 3 = 6	14 ÷ 2 = 7	16 ÷ 2 = 8
12 ÷ 12 = 1	21 ÷ 7 = 3	24 ÷ 3 = 8

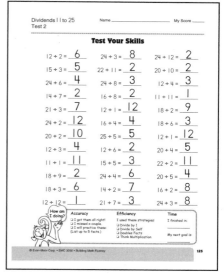

How am I doing? — Accuracy: I got them all right! / I missed a couple. / I will practice these: (List up to 5 facts.) — Efficiency: I used these strategies: Divide by 1 / Divide by Self / Doubles Facts / Think Multiplication — Time: I finished in: My next goal is:

125

Page 126

Dividends 27 to 50 Test 1   Name _____   My Score ____

Test Your Skills

28 ÷ 4 = 7	50 ÷ 10 = 5	36 ÷ 6 = 6
30 ÷ 6 = 5	48 ÷ 8 = 6	40 ÷ 4 = 10
45 ÷ 5 = 9	30 ÷ 5 = 6	42 ÷ 7 = 6
42 ÷ 6 = 7	32 ÷ 4 = 8	36 ÷ 3 = 12
30 ÷ 3 = 10	48 ÷ 4 = 12	27 ÷ 3 = 9
32 ÷ 8 = 4	33 ÷ 3 = 11	44 ÷ 11 = 4
40 ÷ 10 = 4	33 ÷ 11 = 3	36 ÷ 4 = 9
36 ÷ 12 = 3	35 ÷ 7 = 5	40 ÷ 5 = 8
40 ÷ 8 = 5	49 ÷ 7 = 7	28 ÷ 7 = 4
27 ÷ 9 = 3	36 ÷ 9 = 4	44 ÷ 4 = 11
35 ÷ 5 = 7	30 ÷ 10 = 3	48 ÷ 12 = 4
45 ÷ 9 = 5	48 ÷ 12 = 4	50 ÷ 5 = 8

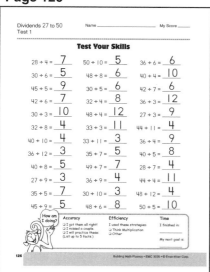

How am I doing? — Accuracy: I got them all right! / I missed a couple. / I will practice these: (List up to 5 facts.) — Efficiency: I used these strategies: Think Multiplication / Other — Time: I finished in: My next goal is:

126

Page 127

Dividends 27 to 50 Test 2   Name _____   My Score ____

Test Your Skills

45 ÷ 5 = 9	28 ÷ 7 = 4	27 ÷ 9 = 3
36 ÷ 6 = 6	40 ÷ 5 = 8	44 ÷ 4 = 11
33 ÷ 11 = 3	30 ÷ 6 = 5	48 ÷ 8 = 6
50 ÷ 5 = 10	32 ÷ 8 = 4	33 ÷ 3 = 11
28 ÷ 4 = 7	42 ÷ 6 = 7	40 ÷ 10 = 4
30 ÷ 5 = 6	40 ÷ 4 = 10	32 ÷ 4 = 8
36 ÷ 3 = 12	44 ÷ 11 = 4	30 ÷ 10 = 3
48 ÷ 6 = 8	36 ÷ 12 = 3	35 ÷ 7 = 5
35 ÷ 5 = 7	36 ÷ 4 = 9	48 ÷ 12 = 4
27 ÷ 3 = 9	49 ÷ 7 = 7	50 ÷ 10 = 5
40 ÷ 8 = 5	36 ÷ 9 = 4	48 ÷ 4 = 12

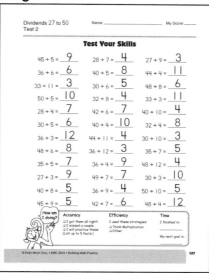

How am I doing? — Accuracy: I got them all right! / I missed a couple. / I will practice these: (List up to 5 facts.) — Efficiency: I used these strategies: Think Multiplication / Other — Time: I finished in: My next goal is:

127

Page 128

Dividends 54 to 81 Test 1   Name _____   My Score ____

Test Your Skills

56 ÷ 7 = 8	80 ÷ 10 = 8	60 ÷ 5 = 12
72 ÷ 12 = 6	63 ÷ 9 = 7	77 ÷ 11 = 7
70 ÷ 7 = 10	56 ÷ 8 = 7	64 ÷ 8 = 8
66 ÷ 11 = 6	54 ÷ 9 = 6	72 ÷ 8 = 9
77 ÷ 7 = 11	63 ÷ 7 = 9	56 ÷ 7 = 8
60 ÷ 10 = 6	66 ÷ 6 = 11	60 ÷ 12 = 5
54 ÷ 6 = 9	72 ÷ 9 = 8	63 ÷ 9 = 7
60 ÷ 5 = 12	55 ÷ 11 = 5	81 ÷ 9 = 9
80 ÷ 8 = 10	60 ÷ 6 = 10	72 ÷ 6 = 12
55 ÷ 5 = 11	70 ÷ 10 = 7	63 ÷ 7 = 9
72 ÷ 8 = 9	64 ÷ 8 = 8	56 ÷ 8 = 7
81 ÷ 9 = 9	54 ÷ 6 = 9	72 ÷ 9 = 8

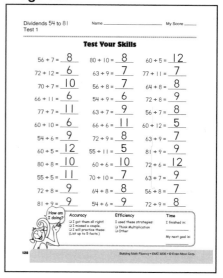

How am I doing? — Accuracy: I got them all right! / I missed a couple. / I will practice these: (List up to 5 facts.) — Efficiency: I used these strategies: Think Multiplication / Other — Time: I finished in: My next goal is:

128

Page 129

Dividends 54 to 81 Test 2   Name _____   My Score ____

Test Your Skills

56 ÷ 7 = 8	63 ÷ 7 = 9	81 ÷ 9 = 9
64 ÷ 8 = 8	72 ÷ 8 = 9	77 ÷ 7 = 11
80 ÷ 10 = 8	56 ÷ 8 = 7	55 ÷ 11 = 5
54 ÷ 6 = 9	70 ÷ 10 = 7	63 ÷ 7 = 9
81 ÷ 9 = 9	55 ÷ 5 = 11	60 ÷ 5 = 12
66 ÷ 11 = 6	60 ÷ 10 = 6	72 ÷ 9 = 8
54 ÷ 9 = 6	60 ÷ 5 = 12	72 ÷ 6 = 12
77 ÷ 11 = 7	72 ÷ 12 = 6	56 ÷ 8 = 8
63 ÷ 9 = 7	54 ÷ 9 = 6	64 ÷ 8 = 8
72 ÷ 6 = 12	60 ÷ 6 = 10	54 ÷ 9 = 7
60 ÷ 12 = 5	80 ÷ 10 = 8	63 ÷ 9 = 7
72 ÷ 12 = 6	72 ÷ 8 = 8	72 ÷ 9 = 8

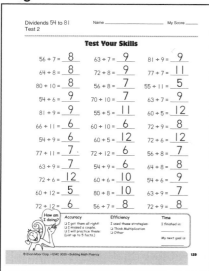

How am I doing? — Accuracy: I got them all right! / I missed a couple. / I will practice these: (List up to 5 facts.) — Efficiency: I used these strategies: Think Multiplication / Other — Time: I finished in: My next goal is:

129

Page 130

Dividends 84 to 144   Name _____   My Score ____

Test Your Skills

110 ÷ 10 = 11	108 ÷ 9 = 12	99 ÷ 9 = 11
84 ÷ 12 = 7	84 ÷ 7 = 12	96 ÷ 12 = 8
108 ÷ 9 = 12	99 ÷ 11 = 9	121 ÷ 11 = 11
90 ÷ 9 = 10	96 ÷ 8 = 12	84 ÷ 7 = 12
132 ÷ 12 = 11	88 ÷ 8 = 11	110 ÷ 10 = 11
108 ÷ 12 = 9	96 ÷ 12 = 8	88 ÷ 11 = 8
144 ÷ 12 = 12	120 ÷ 10 = 12	84 ÷ 12 = 7
84 ÷ 7 = 12	132 ÷ 11 = 12	144 ÷ 12 = 12
90 ÷ 10 = 9	84 ÷ 12 = 7	132 ÷ 12 = 11
120 ÷ 12 = 10	108 ÷ 12 = 9	110 ÷ 11 = 10
99 ÷ 9 = 11	100 ÷ 10 = 10	88 ÷ 11 = 8
110 ÷ 12 = 10	84 ÷ 7 = 12	120 ÷ 10 = 12

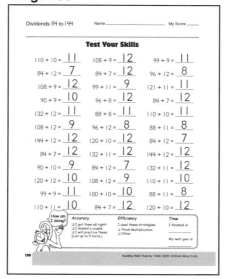

How am I doing? — Accuracy: I got them all right! / I missed a couple. / I will practice these: (List up to 5 facts.) — Efficiency: I used these strategies: Think Multiplication / Other — Time: I finished in: My next goal is:

130

Page 131

Dividends to 81 Review   Name _____   My Score ____

Test Your Skills

4 ÷ 2 = 2	49 ÷ 7 = 7	25 ÷ 5 = 5
12 ÷ 3 = 4	24 ÷ 4 = 6	32 ÷ 4 = 8
30 ÷ 5 = 6	6 ÷ 2 = 3	12 ÷ 2 = 6
18 ÷ 2 = 9	36 ÷ 4 = 9	48 ÷ 6 = 8
42 ÷ 6 = 7	24 ÷ 3 = 8	16 ÷ 2 = 8
20 ÷ 4 = 5	72 ÷ 8 = 9	81 ÷ 9 = 9
27 ÷ 3 = 9	8 ÷ 2 = 4	14 ÷ 2 = 7
40 ÷ 5 = 8	21 ÷ 3 = 7	36 ÷ 6 = 6
18 ÷ 3 = 6	16 ÷ 4 = 4	35 ÷ 5 = 7
64 ÷ 8 = 8	9 ÷ 3 = 3	28 ÷ 4 = 7
24 ÷ 6 = 4	45 ÷ 5 = 9	63 ÷ 9 = 7
54 ÷ 6 = 9	56 ÷ 7 = 8	15 ÷ 3 = 5

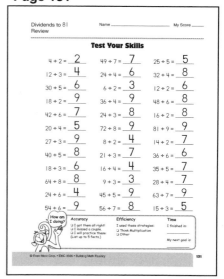

How am I doing? — Accuracy: I got them all right! / I missed a couple. / I will practice these: (List up to 5 facts.) — Efficiency: I used these strategies: Think Multiplication / Other — Time: I finished in: My next goal is:

131

Page 132

Name _____ My Score _____

Test Your Skills

$27 \div 9 = 3$	$54 \div 9 = 6$	$72 \div 9 = 8$
$60 \div 12 = 5$	$144 \div 12 = 12$	$40 \div 8 = 5$
$64 \div 8 = 8$	$132 \div 12 = 11$	$96 \div 12 = 8$
$18 \div 6 = 3$	$108 \div 9 = 12$	$132 \div 11 = 12$
$90 \div 10 = 9$	$72 \div 12 = 6$	$81 \div 9 = 9$
$30 \div 6 = 5$	$21 \div 7 = 3$	$28 \div 7 = 4$
$88 \div 11 = 8$	$20 \div 5 = 4$	$49 \div 7 = 7$
$12 \div 4 = 3$	$84 \div 12 = 7$	$110 \div 10 = 11$
$24 \div 8 = 3$	$63 \div 9 = 7$	$24 \div 6 = 4$
$42 \div 7 = 6$	$48 \div 8 = 6$	$32 \div 8 = 4$
$36 \div 9 = 4$	$99 \div 11 = 9$	$108 \div 12 = 9$
$100 \div 10 = 10$	$15 \div 5 = 3$	$36 \div 9 = 4$

How am I doing?

Accuracy	Efficiency	Time
❑ I got them all right!	I used these strategies:	I finished in:
❑ I missed a couple.	❑ Think Multiplication	
❑ I will practice these:	❑ Other	
(List up to 5 facts.)		My next goal is: